If The
WALLS
Could TALK:
BALTIMORE RAVENS

If These WALLS Could TALK:
BALTIMORE RAVENS

Stories from the
Baltimore Ravens Sideline,
Locker Room, and Press Box

Stan White with Todd Karpovich and Jeff Seidel

TRIUMPH
BOOKS

Library of Congress Cataloging-in-Publication Data
Names: White, Stan, 1949- author. | Karpovich, Todd, author. | Seidel, Jeff, author.
Title: If these walls could talk, Baltimore Ravens : stories from the Baltimore Ravens sideline, locker room, and press box / Stan White with Todd Karpovich and Jeff Seidel.
Description: Chicago, Illinois : Triumph Books, 2017.
Identifiers: LCCN 2017015867 | ISBN 9781629374604 (paperback)
Subjects: LCSH: Baltimore Ravens (Football team)—History. | Baltimore Ravens (Football team)—Anecdotes. | BISAC: SPORTS & RECREATION / Football. | TRAVEL / United States / South / South Atlantic (DC, DE, FL, GA, MD, NC, SC, VA, WV).
Classification: LCC GV956.B3 H45 2017 | DDC 796.357/64097526—dc23 LC record available at https://lccn.loc.gov/2017015867

This book is available in quantity at special discounts for your group or organization. For further information, contact:

Triumph Books LLC
814 North Franklin Street
Chicago, Illinois 60610
(312) 337-0747
www.triumphbooks.com

Printed in U.S.A.
ISBN: 978-1-62937-460-4
Design by Amy Carter
Page Production by Nord Compo
Photos courtesy of Mitchell Layton

CONTENTS

ACKNOWLEDGMENTS

First and foremost, I thank God for this opportunity. I am also grateful to my wife, Jill Karpovich; daughters, Wyeth and Marta; my parents, Phil and Anita Karpovich; and in-laws, Dr. Ed and Jaye Crooks, for their continued support and patience. Thanks to my partners-in-crime, Jeff Seidel and Stan White. Finally, a big thanks to the Ravens for their fair treatment of the media and access to players, coaches, and personnel.

—Todd Karpovich

To Dr. Jack Feldman, Dr. Marc Gertner, and Dr. David Roggen (in alphabetical order), plus the staff at the Alvin & Lois Lapidus Cancer Institute's Outpatient Infusion Center (especially Nurse Julie McNelis, whom I probably drove completely crazy at times) for taking such damn good care of me in 2016. And, of course, my marvelous family, especially my wife (Nadine), kids (Kara and Zach), mom (Elaine), in-laws (Muriel and Leroy Handwerger), and cats (Buddy, Albie) for the much-needed strength they gave me. Yes, even the cats. Plus, cheers to my wonderful co-authors, Todd Karpovich and Stan White. Also, thanks so very much to Michelle Bruton and Noah Amstadter at Triumph Books, who helped make this all happen and guided us along. We were lucky to have them.

—Jeff Seidel

I dedicate this book first to my two fathers, God the Father and my Dad, Bill White, then to my mother, Marj, who I lost eight years ago and I miss every day. Then to my wife of 44 years, Patty, and to my three kids and eight (soon-to-be-nine) grandkids. I love all of you with all my heart.

—Stan White

INTRODUCTION

Icame to Baltimore in 1972 because of football, as the 17th-round draft choice of the Baltimore Colts out of Ohio State—No. 438 out of 442 players drafted that year. The first person I lined up against in training camp was tight end John Mackey in the old Oklahoma drill. The quarterback was Johnny Unitas. Somehow, I made the 40-man roster that season and survived the first year.

Overall, I was lucky enough to play for 13 years in professional football, the first eight of which came in Baltimore. I always kept my home in Baltimore even as I traveled to Detroit, Chicago, and Arizona while playing in those cities. The Colts leaving in 1984 the way they did really devastated the city and the state. They loved football in Baltimore and Maryland—and the Colts in particular. The next 13 years were spent trying to get an NFL team back to Charm City.

When I heard the news that the Browns might be moving to Baltimore, I called owner Art Modell at his home in Cleveland the night before he flew to Baltimore to announce the move. He wouldn't confirm anything. He just said, "Stan, I'll see you tomorrow." He never returned to Cleveland after that day.

Baltimore had a team again. I had a team again. My kids had a team to grow up with. My son was 13, and he got to be on the sidelines running Polaroid pictures coming from the press box to the sidelines on a clothesline. He also worked in the press box as a high school kid. He went to Super Bowl XXXV—and the Super Bowl victory party after the game. He eventually played football at Ohio State, winning a National Championship and being a first-team Academic All-American fullback.

My kids and everyone else in Maryland have had their lives so enriched by the Baltimore Ravens. My daughter is a huge Ravens fan. She and her husband have five boys. They took three of them to the Ravens' second Super Bowl win in Super Bowl XLVII. They were sitting in the end zone where the Ravens executed a last goal-line stand in the final moments to lock up a victory over the 49ers. Coach John Harbaugh beating his brother, Jim, was really something. I got to interview their father, Jack, live on WBAL on the field after the game.

I also have been a high school coach for the last 20 years. The effect the Ravens have had on high school football in Maryland has been dramatic since they've been here. When the Ravens first came there were about 20 Division I college recruits a year. Now, that number is in the hundreds. The Ravens have done so much for football and for this area, and I'm glad to have seen it happen.

—*Stan White*

CHAPTER 1
HEARTBREAK AND HOPE

On March 28, 1984, about a dozen Mayflower moving trucks weathered a snow storm to pick up equipment at the Baltimore Colts training facility in Owings Mills, Maryland. Under the cover of darkness, the Colts—a longtime fixture in the local community—were being whisked away to Indianapolis. Baltimore Mayor William Donald Schaefer and local residents could only watch helplessly as their beloved franchise was taken from them with no recourse from the NFL. It would be 12 years before Baltimore would play another NFL game.

The sight of those Mayflower trucks broke the hearts of Colts fans, who had become disenchanted with the team under the tumultuous ownership of Robert Irsay. As attendance at Colts games dwindled, the embattled owner also openly courted other cities—Phoenix, Memphis, and Jacksonville—as potential landing spots for the franchise. His relationships with Baltimore, local politicians, and the media continued to get worse for Irsay, who reportedly once called the Colts sideline during a regular season game to "suggest" a play for the offense.

Despite the acrimony, no one had expected that Irsay would abruptly wrestle the team away and set up shop 600 miles away in Indiana. It was a heartbreak many people in Baltimore would never get over. For years, thousands of Colts fans flocked to Memorial Stadium on 33rd Street. The stadium became known as the "World's Largest Outdoor Insane Asylum" because of the fans' passion. Players such as Johnny Unitas, Art Donovan, and Ray Berry became local heroes. Suddenly, the Colts were now gone and there was a void on Sundays—fall afternoons that could not be filled.

Unitas and many other former Baltimore Colts players didn't want to be affiliated with the team when it moved to Indianapolis. It left a deep scar.

"The tradition is in Baltimore," the late Unitas told the *Los Angeles Times* in 1996 when the Colts were playing the Steelers for the AFC Championship. "There is no reason for any of us who played for Baltimore to be with Indianapolis. They have never invited me there with a personal invitation, but if they had, I would have said, 'Thank you, but no thanks.' The Colts' name belongs in Baltimore, just like the Rams' name belongs in Los Angeles. If the commissioner had any power whatsoever, he would petition the owners to vote in that fashion.... What I think is important is for Baltimore to have a franchise. It's important for the NFL too. Baltimore was one of the dominating teams in the NFL, one that helped the NFL to gain the prominence that it has."

When the Colts left Baltimore, the NFL assumed that many football fans in Baltimore would simply embrace the Washington Redskins, who played about 40 miles away at RFK Stadium. The league's officials and owners were wrong. Instead of fans supporting the Redskins, a growing disdain evolved against the team in Baltimore because the local community felt the franchise was being forced on them. Baltimore had its own NFL team for too long to simply embrace another franchise, especially in Washington, which had already taken its basketball team, the Bullets. What Baltimore really wanted was its Colts back, but it became increasingly clear that it was not going to happen.

To further add to the indignity, Irsay also took the Colts' colors and history with him to Indianapolis. Those artifacts, the iconic horseshoe, and records would never return. Baltimore later landed a Canadian Football League franchise called the Stallions in 1994. Just one year later, they became the first American team to win the Grey Cup. While the Stallions had a loyal following, the CFL most certainly was not the NFL. The team did, however, manage to fill some of the void while Baltimore worked to land an NFL team.

Over the next decade, Baltimore became a valuable bargaining chip for other NFL owners who wanted new stadium deals in their cities. If their respective cities did not want to help with public financing, the officials in Baltimore were more than happy to help land a new team. This wasn't a veiled threat. Baltimore desperately wanted to be back in the NFL and the financial support was sincere. The Baltimore Colts Marching Band even stayed active with the hope they would have a new team to support and to show other owners that their enthusiasm for the NFL didn't wane. Meanwhile, the state of Maryland did indeed have plans in place for a new stadium if an NFL team was willing to relocate. The Cardinals and Rams each flirted with Baltimore, but nothing ever came to fruition. The hopes for landing an NFL team grew dimmer each passing year, and some paranoia even began to set in.

Baltimore was that shell-shocked by the loss of the Colts, fears began to arise that the Orioles might follow them, perhaps to Washington. As a result, the city was more than happy to build the Orioles a shiny new stadium in downtown Baltimore, just a few miles from the aging Memorial Stadium. This paved the way for the construction of Oriole Park at Camden Yards, which became the crown jewel of baseball stadiums and revolutionized architecture. Since then, the Orioles have never been a threat to flee to another city, and they led Major League Baseball in attendance for several years in the 1990s. Today, Camden Yards remains a model stadium that other MLB cities have tried to emulate.

With a stroke of luck, Baltimore's NFL dreams had new life in 1993 when the NFL announced the league would expand by two teams for the first time since 1976. Baltimore had put together one of the strongest proposals of the potential landing of the two spots for the new franchise. Shirts that said GIVE BALTIMORE THE BALL were ubiquitous around the city. Charlotte, St. Louis, Memphis, and Jacksonville also were bidding for franchises. Baltimore, however, was the only city with three ownership groups vying for the franchise. The city also had all the pieces in place for a new stadium.

On August 27, 1992, 60,021 fans filled Memorial Stadium for a preseason game between the New Orleans Saints and the Miami Dolphins. Fans chanted in unison, "We want a team." The city wanted to show the NFL its interest in getting the expansion team was above and beyond the other competing cities. "Their enthusiasm for football is great and their turnout tonight really shows that," said Roger Goodell, who was then vice president of operations for the NFL.

Nonetheless, the first wave of further disappointment arrived on October 26, 1993, when NFL owners unanimously supported Carolina as the league's 29th NFL franchise. The move made sense geographically, because there was no NFL franchise in the southeast part of the United States from Washington to Tampa Bay. The Carolina Panthers certainly filled a void for the NFL, and there was little surprise they were granted a franchise. A new stadium in Charlotte certainly helped the case for the Carolina Panthers' ownership group headed by Jerry Richardson.

Despite the setback, Baltimore was not totally discouraged, because there was still an opportunity to land the other franchise. The city had a bigger market than Jacksonville, a better stadium deal than Memphis, and did not have any litigation concerns like St. Louis. However, there was already talk about Redskins owner Jack Kent Cooke lobbying against a team in Baltimore because of the close proximity to his franchise. The impression was that he wanted to control both markets despite there being little support for his team in Baltimore. This fueled even more backlash against the Redskins. Nonetheless, the ownership groups in Maryland were confident with the proposals and remained optimistic they would land the second expansion franchise.

Everything came to a screeching halt on November 30, 1993. The NFL owners made a surprise move and selected Jacksonville as the league's 30th franchise. Jacksonville had dropped out of the bidding the previous year because the ownership group had trouble negotiating a stadium deal with the city. Those issues were eventually ironed out, but Jacksonville was still widely considered a long shot behind Baltimore and St. Louis to land the expansion franchise. Nonetheless, the owners were confident a team in Jacksonville would further fill the void in the southeastern market of the U.S. "It became clear to the committees that the Southeast has become a tremendous area for expansion," then-NFL Commissioner Paul Tagliabue said about the announcement.

The Carolina Panthers and Jacksonville Jaguars would begin play in 1995. Baltimore was reeling again. One of the potential owners for an expansion team in Baltimore was Malcolm Glazer, who would eventually lead the ownership group in Tampa. His disappointment was clear. "I'm going home and cry," Glazer told the *New York Times* after hearing the announcement. "I feel very sad. Baltimore has a group of fans you can't find anywhere else in America."

Finally, officials in Baltimore had come to the conclusion that the NFL was not going to give them a team. If the city wanted a franchise, then it would have to use the same tactics as Indianapolis—lure an existing one. It was not an ideal situation, but there was simply no other way. Baltimore found the perfect partner in the Cleveland Browns' Art Modell, an old-school owner with long ties to the league who was having trouble in his adopted city.

Modell had been telling Cleveland officials that the Browns needed a new stadium to not only compete for championships, but to remain fiscally viable. Modell watched the Indians in MLB and the NBA's Cavaliers get shiny new facilities. Cleveland also built the Rock & Roll Hall of Fame on the shores of Lake Erie that was a national attraction. The Browns, however, were left out in the cold. The City of Cleveland argued that fans regularly filled the stadium for Browns home games and that was enough to keep the team financially viable. If the franchise was struggling, then it was Modell's own financial ineptness that was the source of the problems. A standoff was inevitable, and it seemed neither side was going to blink.

John Moag was the chairman of Maryland Stadium Authority at the time. That group was founded in 1986 to build, manage, and maintain stadium facilities across Maryland. The Maryland Stadium Authority was desperate to add an NFL facility to its portfolio. Moag saw the dilemma between Modell and the City of Cleveland as an opportunity to land a franchise. Moag and other state officials eventually put together a deal Modell couldn't refuse. If the Browns would relocate, Baltimore agreed to build a $200 million publicly financed stadium that would become one of the best facilities in the entire NFL. The relocated franchise would not have to pay any rent, and it could collect profits from all concessions, parking, and signage. It was a sweetheart deal from a city that was ready to play ball.

In addition, Modell's franchise would annually earn millions of dollars from the sale of luxury suites and club seats. Season ticket sales would also help pay for a new training complex. Not seeing any hope in striking an agreement in Cleveland, Modell decided to make a bold move. A deal to bring the Browns to Baltimore was consummated on October 27, 1995, on a private jet at Baltimore-Washington International Airport. Modell had hoped to withhold the news until after the regular season, so his players would not be utterly distracted, and perhaps harassed, by the announcement. However, the rumor mill was already swirling. As a result, a formal press conference was announced at Baltimore's Inner Harbor on November 6, 1995, to make the deal public and official. The Browns were indeed coming to Baltimore, breaking the hearts of thousands of Clevelanders—much like the Colts fans a decade earlier.

Modell was contrite and Maryland state officials, at least most of them, tried to subdue their glee at the press conference. "I know what you went through 11 years ago, because that is exactly what is happening in Cleveland right now," Modell told a crowd of more than 200 people who gathered on the blustery fall day. "I am deeply, deeply sorry from the bottom of my heart."

Being contrite, however, wasn't good enough for the folks in Ohio. Modell was vilified for taking the Browns away. The City of Cleveland filed a lawsuit to keep the team. There was outrage around the country by the national media. How could a venerable franchise like the Cleveland Browns relocate? It almost seemed preposterous. Cleveland, much like Green Bay and Pittsburgh, represented the old guard of the NFL. The backlash was nonstop, but neither Modell nor the City of Baltimore would back down. This was the only way the city would get a team, and it was not going to let go.

Cleveland was not going down without a fight. "We have not been dealt with fairly; we have not been dealt with honestly," Mayor Michael White said at the time. "And we are not going to go away. We have been wronged. I did not come here to go through the motions. We are going to do what it takes. The principle of how we've been treated is worth fighting for." That rallying cry was echoed across northeast Ohio and into other parts of the country.

After much haggling and angst, a compromise was eventually struck. Modell and his franchise would indeed relocate to Baltimore. To help expedite the process, the state of Maryland dropped a $36 million antitrust lawsuit it had filed against the NFL. To help pacify the Redskins, Maryland lawmakers agreed to provide $73 million toward that franchise's proposed facility in Prince George's County—widely regarded as a suburb of Washington. However, the Browns' history and colors would remain in Cleveland. The Browns franchise would also be resurrected and play in a new luxury stadium with the help of the NFL. The new Baltimore franchise would have to create its own identity to begin play for the 1996 season. That was just fine for the people in Maryland who still had some guilt about the relocation of the team. The Browns' name and colors would be a constant reminder of that.

The new team in Baltimore initially wore black and white uniforms for offseason activities. After two months of research, panel discussions, focus groups, and fan polling, the team announced on March 29, 1996, that the franchise would be called the Ravens, taken from the Edgar Allan Poe poem "The Raven," which tells the story of a mysterious bird tormenting a grieving man. A telephone poll by the *Baltimore Sun* received a record number of calls supporting that name. Poe wrote many of his poems in Baltimore and died in the city on October 7, 1849. He is buried on the grounds of Westminster Hall and Burying Ground, which is part of the University of Maryland School of Law in Baltimore. Even though he was born in Boston, Poe remains one of Baltimore's favorite adopted sons. His macabre nature perfectly fit the gritty city.

"It's a strong nickname that is not common to teams at any level, and it means something historically to this community," said the late David Modell, the son of the owner and the then-assistant to the president.

On June 5, the team announced its colors would be black, purple, and metallic gold. That worked perfectly for the City of Baltimore. The wounds from losing the Colts would sting "nevermore."

The NFL was finally back.

CHAPTER 2
WELCOME TO BALTIMORE

Ted Marchibroda was the team's first head coach. He ran the Ravens from 1996 to 1998 but never could make the team a winner. He also coached the Baltimore Colts in the late '70s and took that team to the playoffs three consecutive years. Brian Billick replaced Marchibroda in January 1999 with the Ravens and won a Super Bowl two seasons later.

The Baltimore Ravens opened the regular season to much fanfare on September 1, 1996. Fans flocked to 33rd Street in droves to greet the new franchise in its inaugural game against the Oakland Raiders. Many of the former Baltimore Colts were on hand to participate in pre-game ceremonies, including Johnny Unitas and Art Donovan. The team rewarded the crowd of 64,124—the largest in Memorial Stadium's 42-year history—with a 19–14 victory. Ravens quarterback Vinny Testaverde scored the team's first touchdown on a nine-yard run that sent the stadium into a frenzy reminiscent of the old Colts days.

This game, however, was not your usual regular season opener. The impact and historical importance of the day was not lost on the Ravens players, many of whom spent a miserable prior season in Cleveland as a lame duck franchise. After the game, Testaverde paid homage to Unitas and the storied football history in Baltimore. "Just knowing that he was here today, a legend with the great years he had in Baltimore, it's just a great beginning for this franchise," Testaverde said after the game. The victory over the Raiders, however, was one of the few highlights of that season.

Playing under former Colts coach Ted Marchibroda, the Ravens went just 4–12. Despite that poor record, Baltimore was mostly competitive, holding a second-half lead in 10 of their final 11 games. The Ravens, however, managed to win just two of those matchups. The defense simply struggled to close out games. Still, many of the local fans were not overly concerned about the team's record in that first season. The city was just happy to have the NFL back on Sunday afternoons.

The Ravens finished 0–8 on the road but 4–4 at home. Along with the opening-day victory, another signature win at Memorial

Stadium arrived on December 1, 1996, when the Ravens upset the Pittsburgh Steelers 31–17 on a cold and rainy afternoon. The win was even sweeter because the thousands of Steelers fans who managed to secure tickets and wave their Terrible Towels went home wet and disappointed. The team's No. 1 draft pick, offensive tackle Jonathan Ogden, scored his first career touchdown on a 1-yard pass from Testaverde. That would help set the stage for a long-standing division rivalry with Pittsburgh, which would later become the most heated in the NFL.

The Ravens finished last in the AFC Central behind the Steelers, Jaguars, Bengals, and Houston Oilers that season. However, the season was not a total disappointment. Baltimore had an explosive, entertaining offense, which finished sixth overall in the NFL. The strong-armed Testaverde was named to the Pro Bowl after throwing for 4,177 yards and 33 touchdowns. Two other players, Michael Jackson and Derrick Alexander, had more than 1,000 receiving yards apiece and combined for 23 touchdown receptions. It was a fun, high-flying offense.

The other side of the ball was a different matter, as the Ravens defense had trouble stopping any of its opponents. Baltimore finished the season ranked 28 out of 30 teams for total defense, ahead of just the Falcons and Jets. The Ravens allowed 27.6 points per game, which was third-worst in the NFL. However, the high-scoring games made for some entertaining football on Sunday afternoons. The team also had some solid young players on defense, so there was hope for future improvement.

More importantly, though, the team was embraced by the Baltimore community. The Ravens sold out every game that season, including both preseason matchups. In fact, the team sold more than 50,000 season tickets the first 14 days they became available. There were some initial concerns about how the Baltimore fans would accept the franchise because of the way it had been taken from Cleveland. Even though many of these fans still complained about how the Colts were stolen, there was some sense of guilt about using the same tactic to get the Browns. It didn't help that the Ravens were continuously criticized by the national media for "stealing" the Browns. The fact that the Browns' colors and history remained in Cleveland helped matters.

David Ginsburg covered the Ravens for the Associated Press since the inaugural season. He remembers the team being an anomaly at first because of the relocations.

"My memory of that season was that the Ravens had some trouble drumming up interest because the city was a bit embarrassed about taking the team out of Cleveland the way Indy took the Colts," Ginsburg said. "The team played at shitty Memorial Stadium and many tickets were available outside the gates. The team was more of a curiosity than a winner."

NBC analyst Bob Trumpy was one of the most vocal critics of the new Ravens. In a column for *Inside Sports*, Trumpy wrote, "I despise the whole concept of the Baltimore Ravens.... This team will be hated everywhere outside of Baltimore.... Art Modell's actions were criminal.... I see nothing but gloom and doom for this franchise." He ended the missive by concluding, "I wish the Ravens high winds and muddy fields; I wish them empty roads to and from the ballpark; I wish them cold hot dogs. I wish them nothing but bad."

Those comments created a stir in the Baltimore community. Milton Kent, a writer for the *Baltimore Sun* at the time, even contacted Trumpy about the comments and offered him an opportunity to perhaps soften that stance. Trumpy, however, was unrepentant, but he did acknowledge the ire was mainly aimed at Art Modell and not Baltimore.

"Look, I'm not going to plead my case to the Baltimore fans," Trumpy told Kent. "I'm not interested in doing that. I owe them no apologies. I think a lot of these things happen where one person reads an article, reports it to another person, and it's passed along by a third, and suddenly what's talked about is not, in fact, in the article."

The Ravens were also creating their own identity, distancing themselves from the move. The purple, black, and metallic gold colors were the polar opposite of the Browns' orange and brown. The Ravens also kept close ties with several former Colts players to help lure some of the older fans who harkened back to those glory days. It was also a perfect way to seamlessly transition from the past to the present and future. Cleveland had promised a new team, so eventually the backlash from the move would subside, especially when the new Browns began play in 1999. The NFL had set up Cleveland with a sweet deal for a new stadium and the cards were in place for that franchise to thrive. The new team in Cleveland would also help heal some of the wounds from the move.

Also, the Ravens were in the process of building a new, state-of-the-art stadium adjacent to Camden Yards. The neighboring stadiums were expected to create a buzzing sports complex in the heart of downtown Baltimore. This was not only enticing to fans, but a boon to downtown businesses. There certainly was room for two professional franchises in the Baltimore market. The Ravens had a training facility in Owings Mills and were slowly gaining traction in the community. The team also held practices at a local small college in Westminster, Maryland, where fans could interact with the players. The NFL was once again a fixture in Baltimore. The Ravens were strategically planning a future for long-term success, which would not come easily.

STAN'S SIDEBAR

ON THE CITY TAKING TO THE NEW TEAM

It did take awhile. I think right away younger people were really happy to have a team. Some of the older people I think were waiting. I think if they named them the Colts, it would have been a lot easier for everybody to accept. But at first, they were going to be the Browns, if you remember. It was going to be the Baltimore Browns. I had talked to Art Modell several times during that process, because I got to know him due to my relationship on the Players Association to the owners. I had called him at his house the night before he came here to say, "Is this really going to happen?" And he said, "Stan, I'll be there tomorrow, that's all I know." I don't think he ever set foot back in Ohio again after that night. I think that was his last night.

When he did the press conference here, Art knew there were going to be a lot of bad feelings back in Cleveland. My family's from the area. I grew up watching them. They still have hard feelings about us taking their team, especially after somebody had taken ours, and we felt so bad about that. It took a while for a lot of the old Colts fans. They sort of hung on to what they grew up with. You can't blame them for that. But most of them I know now have changed, because their kids and then their grandchildren have hooked on to the Ravens. They've softened quite a bit on that. There's a few who still remember the Colts. They loved their time with the Colts but most of them have not let that stop them from being Ravens fans. When they got the new stadium, I think that was a brand-new start. In the old stadium, it sort of brought back a lot of memories. I remember Bob Costas coming out and talking about how Baltimore stole the team just like it was stolen from them, and they should be ashamed and all that stuff.

Once they moved to the new stadium, I think everybody was used to the term *Ravens*, and they were starting to build a team. I think it was really the new stadium that catapulted them into being accepted in this town. At first it was weird. It was different. It was a team you'd never seen before, a logo you'd never seen, a name you'd never seen before, players that you didn't know. It was all new, but it was the satisfaction of having a team, finally having a team back. So that was the genesis of everything else.

They got their team back. They're an NFL city again. By the time they got that new stadium, I think the Ravens were part of the fabric here.

CHAPTER 3

THE CORNERSTONES OF THE FRANCHISE

Much of the Ravens' long-term success was built around their first-ever draft in 1996. With a pair of first-round selections that year, it was paramount the team make the best possible selections to put them on a winning path. Whiffing on a first-round pick can set a franchise back for years. It was during this draft that Baltimore general manager Ozzie Newsome began to earn a reputation as one of the best in the business in regard to evaluating players. The Ravens have been able to grab several game-changing players in the NFL draft, but 1996 might have been their best performance.

The Ravens were able to get the two first-round picks because of a trade the Cleveland Browns made the prior season. The Browns sent the 10th overall pick in 1995 draft to San Francisco in exchange for three picks that same year. The deal also involved the 49ers' first-round selection in 1996. As a result of the move, the Ravens were able to take full advantage. Baltimore had the fourth overall pick of the 1996 draft because of the Browns' 5–11 record the previous year. Baltimore also had the 26th overall pick courtesy of the trade with San Francisco. It was an enviable position because that draft was stocked with talent.

The Ravens sorely needed to take advantage of that opportunity…and they did, in a big way.

With the fourth overall pick, Baltimore took offensive tackle Jonathan Ogden from UCLA. Ogden hailed from Washington, D.C., and prepped at St. Albans School, so there was already some familiarity with the area. As a UCLA Bruin, he established himself as the top offensive lineman in the country. Ogden's imposing 6'9", 345-pound frame allowed him to maul opposing defenders, and he was rarely beaten for a sack.

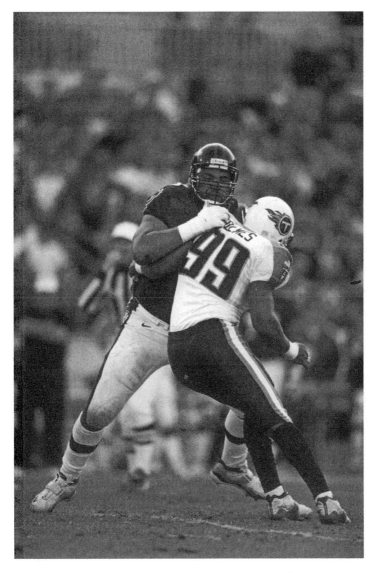

Jonathan Ogden was the team's first draft choice after moving to Baltimore before the 1996 season, and what a pick he turned out to be, giving them a left tackle for the ages. Ogden had it all—size, speed, quickness, and agility—and he anchored the line for years. He later made the NFL Hall of Fame, a pick that surprised no one.

Bobb McKittrick, a former San Francisco 49ers offensive-line coach, hailed Ogden as "the No. 1 offensive-line prospect ever." Ogden lived up to those lofty expectations. Over his 12-year career, Ogden appeared in 177 games, played in 11 Pro Bowls, and was named to nine All-Pro teams—and all with the Ravens. He was voted into the NFL Hall of Fame in 2013.

"Everyone had me going to Arizona with the third pick and they wound up picking [defensive end] Simeon Rice," Ogden told the NFL Network prior to his being inducted into the Pro Football Hall of Fame. "I was a little disconcerted, but not too much. Then I remember the phone ringing, and it was Ozzie Newsome for me. He said, 'Are you ready to become a Baltimore Raven?' I said, 'Let's do it, man. Let's build something special down there in Baltimore.'"

The Ravens had contemplated taking troubled Nebraska running back Lawrence Phillips, but Newsome, who was the director of football operations at the time, decided to stick to his draft board and selected Ogden. Phillips played just three seasons in the NFL and tragically committed suicide in prison in 2016. The Ravens have never wavered from taking the best player available according to their draft board. It is a philosophy that has served them well over the years. This strategy has made their scouting department a model to replicate among other NFL teams. Newsome was eventually named general manager—a promotion he directly attributes to the selection of Ogden in that draft.

"Jonathan is the foundation of this franchise," Newsome told ESPN. "If we don't pick Jonathan Ogden with that first pick, I may not have this job."

The Ravens' second pick in the first round proved to be equally as shrewd. With the 26th overall selection, Baltimore chose linebacker Ray Lewis from the University of Miami. Lewis eventually changed the face of the franchise. Despite a stellar college career, Lewis was widely regarded as being undersized at 6'0"and 220 pounds. Somehow, his heart and drive were underestimated. His leadership skills were also the best of any player in the draft.

Despite the intangibles, the Ravens still had their sights set on linebacker Reggie Brown of Texas A&M. However, Brown went to the Lions with the 17th overall pick. Lewis was still there at No. 26 and the Ravens jumped on him. While ESPN draft expert Mel Kiper acknowledged that Lewis was indeed on the smaller size, he said the linebacker had "tremendous instincts, range, [and] excellent form." Lewis ultimately became one of the best linebackers to ever play the game.

Lewis made an immediate impact in his rookie year with Baltimore. In the season opener against the Raiders, Lewis played like a veteran and led the team with seven tackles. He also got his first career interception. That performance earned him the AFC Defensive Player of the Week. In all, Lewis appeared in 14 games, including 13 starts, and finished with a team-high 142 tackles that season. For that dominant performance, he was named to *USA Today*'s All-Rookie Team and showed all of the signs that he was the long-term answer at middle linebacker.

Lewis got better with each passing year. By the time he retired in 2012, he had been invited to 13 Pro Bowls and was a two-time NFL Defensive Player of the Year (2000 and 2003). He is just the sixth player in NFL history to win that award multiple times, along with Lawrence Taylor, Joe Greene, Mike Singletary, Bruce

Smith, and Reggie White. Lewis was named the MVP of Super Bowl XXXV. He also overcame several controversies and is widely regarded as the best player in the history of the Baltimore Ravens. Lewis was the face of the franchise in his 17 years with the team. His signature pregame dance fired up the crowd and was imitated by other players and even celebrities. Lewis would eventually have a statue of his likeness resurrected outside M&T Bank Stadium, right next to the beloved Johnny Unitas, forever immortalized in Baltimore

Lewis did experience controversy in Baltimore. In 2000, a fight broke out following a party after Super Bowl XXXIV in Atlanta where two people, Jacinth Baker and Richard Lollar, were stabbed to death. Lewis was eventually indicted on murder and aggravated-assault charges before eventually pleading guilty to a misdemeanor charge of obstruction of justice in exchange for the testimony. That case has never been solved and it would follow Lewis for much of his NFL career. Still, he returned to the field after the trial and was dominant again. His legendary status in Baltimore would never be doubted. While Harbaugh was impressed by Lewis as a player, he respected him even more for his spirituality and faith in God.

"If you're going to talk about the Ray thing, you want to ask about it, then the answer's got to be faith," Harbaugh said about Lewis after the player decided to retire. "Ray is driven by spirituality and faith and that's what he draws on and that's where his strength comes from. So if you really want to know, that's what he's tapping into and that's what makes it so beautiful and so perfect."

In that first draft, Baltimore also was able to get several other stellar playmakers that made an impact for the team. Jermaine

Lewis, who was picked in the fifth round, was a Pro Bowl returner and scored a touchdown on a kickoff in Super Bowl XXXV. A second-round pick, DeRon Jenkins spent four years at cornerback with the team. "Whatever comes of the history of the Ravens in Baltimore, that [draft] day will forever be the reason why this franchise is where it's at," Lewis said. "It was all because of the genius of Ozzie Newsome."

The Ravens certainly took their lumps in their inaugural season as they found their footing in a new city that was slowly warming up to the idea of having another city's franchise. Still, a foundation was in place for further strides and bigger success. The key was maintaining the sell-out crowds as the losses on the field mounted. A pending new downtown stadium and a solid core of young players, most notably Lewis and Ogden, provided optimism that would soon be rewarded.

At the time, though, few experts predicted that duo would have such stellar careers, mainly because of the team's struggles that season. On first glance, Ogden and Lewis appeared to be a couple of rookies that were just beginning to learn about the nuances of playing in the NFL. Ogden had not even taken over his natural position at left tackle. He played left guard as he learned firsthand about the speed and power of the typical NFL defender. And Lewis was part of a struggling defense that had trouble stopping anyone, allowing close to 30 points per game. Still, he managed to shine for much of the season.

"The Ravens defense was horrible that year, and Ogden started his career at guard because Tony Jones was at left tackle," Associated Press sportswriter David Ginsburg said. "It did not appear early that either of them would end up in the Hall of Fame."

ON OZZIE NEWSOME AND TED MARCHIBRODA

Ozzie has been unbelievably successful as a player. I played against him in his rookie year with the Cleveland Browns. He was a rookie tight end that had just converted from wide receiver. As a linebacker, you were saying, "Oh, this is good; he's not a blocker." But you could tell he was going to be an unbelievable receiver at tight end. He got better at blocking and doing those things, too. Obviously, he was a Hall of Fame player. I grew up in Cleveland, so the Browns were my team. I grew up going to watch them as kids. Ozzie was just a great player, and then he started coaching. He actually coached for a couple years under Bill Belichick, learned from him, went into the front office, and got his first real opportunity when they came here.

Art appointed Ozzie the general manager. He showed his mettle in that first draft, insisting they take Jonathan Ogden, not Lawrence Phillips, with that fourth pick of that first draft. And when you start off with two Hall of Famers in your first two picks and go to the Super Bowl a couple of years later, that's a pretty good way to start your career. He's just built on that. He's behind the scenes. You don't hear him on talk shows. I can't get to him to give interviews. I say hi to him and we talk about college football a lot. He stays out of the spotlight. He does not want the spotlight, but he gets the spotlight because he's been so successful. I mean, he'll be a Hall of Fame general manager on top of being a Hall of Fame player. That doesn't happen very often.

If you compare his drafts to everybody else's—and people don't do that—it's who you get when. It's how you build a team. They've been a perennial playoff contender, and what more could you ask? There are not very many teams that can say they're perennial playoff contenders. The draft's been the Ravens' foundation. The draft is what has made this team great. It's about home-grown players and how many Pro Bowls they've played in, and how many games they've won. I don't even know if New England can match up.

Ted Marchibroda didn't have the players. It was basically an expansion franchise. It was almost starting over. They felt Ted was perfect because he had been a coach here before, had been a successful coach at Indianapolis, had been to the Super Bowl with Buffalo three or four times as their offensive coordinator, so they felt he'd be the perfect fit to come back here and coach again. He probably was. They needed somebody like that to start the building process who was willing to go through and take the lumps. He came here in '75 and we were 2–12 the year before and started off 1–4 and then won nine straight games. He had success early the first time he was here. I'm sure he was hoping for that, and they got Vinny Testaverde at quarterback, which gave them potential. But they just didn't have any defense at that point.

I think Ted was a good fit for that situation, and the Ravens knew they had to move on after that third year. He was looked at as more of an old-school coach. The players thought he practiced them too hard when actually he was a lot less of an old-school coach than when he was with the old Colts. In fact, he apologized to some of us because he had practiced us so hard. Today it's a whole different way of preparing for a season, practicing and everything else.

The players didn't like the way Ted practiced. They thought he was too hard on them. In terms of the Super Bowl two years later, that was the foundation. Brian Billick came in and really, the only change was quarterback. They went through about two or three quarterbacks, and finally Trent Dilfer led them to the Super Bowl, and their defense and kicking game won it for them.

STAN'S SIDEBAR

ON JONATHAN OGDEN

Ogden was a freak, athletically. I remember seeing the films of him at UCLA where he'd be out pulling around like a guard. He had that ability to pull and be able to block people in space like the old-fashioned pulling guards from Green Bay. You watch tackles when they get to that second level, who have a hard time blocking guys in space. He didn't; he had a great center of gravity, he had great feet, he had a great disposition, and he was powerful because of his size. He had everything you wanted in an offensive tackle, plus he loved football.

If you don't have a great quarterback, you better have a great line and a great running back—and a great defense—and I think they did. Even talking now to defensive coordinator Dean Pees, he still comes back to stopping the run, making tackles in the open field, winning at the line of scrimmage. Ogden is up there with a guy named Anthony Munoz who played for the Cincinnati Bengals. He was the only offensive lineman, maybe he and John Hannah, that defensive linemen were afraid of—afraid that he would hurt them. He was that good. As good an athlete as

Anthony was, Jon was probably a better athlete, as far as getting out in open space and doing things.

When you have a good line, even with the Ravens right now, it's important. When you've got a line up front, you can get by. But if you have a great quarterback and a line, then you're in really good shape. You had Ray Lewis on defense and then after the first Super Bowl, Ed Reed came in. So between those two, you had two of the great players of all time defensively, anchoring the front seven and the back seven.

CHAPTER 4
BRIAN BILLICK

Brian Billick took over as head coach in the team's fourth season. They were Super Bowl champions in his second season. He made them play tough yet let them be wild. You could talk the talk but you better walk the walk. The team did plenty of both, especially on defense—a big reason teams did not like to see the Ravens on their schedules.

The Ravens decided to part ways with coach Ted Marchibroda in 1998 after three seasons and a 16–31–1 record. Despite the losing record, Marchibroda did a solid job bridging the gap to a new era for the franchise and steering it through the turmoil of the move from Cleveland. Marchibroda also remained revered in the local community as the former head coach of the Baltimore Colts from 1975 to '79, winning three division titles. After the Ravens, Marchibroda retired from coaching and became a broadcaster for the Indianapolis Colts. He died of natural causes at his home in Weems, Virginia, on January 16, 2016, at the age of 84.

"Ted is a founding father of the Ravens. He was a tough man with a gentle soul," Newsome said in a statement. "In a way, he set the Ravens' path. He wanted players who owned what he called 'a football temperament.' Those are players who love all aspects of the game—the mental part, lifting weights, practice, and the physicality. That eventually became what we now call 'Playing Like a Raven.'"

After Marchibroda left the team, the Ravens were challenged to find the right leader to move the franchise in a positive direction. Modell and Newsome considered several high-profile candidates. At the top of the list were Mike Holmgren, who had won a Super Bowl as the head coach of the Green Bay Packers, and George Seifert, who won a title in San Francisco. Holmgren, however, decided to coach the Seattle Seahawks, while Seifert took a job with Carolina. Other candidates Baltimore considered were Steelers defensive coordinator Jim Haslett and Eagles defensive coordinator Emmitt Thomas.

Newsome and the rest of the front office, however, were highly impressed with Brian Billick, the offensive coordinator for the record-setting Minnesota Vikings. With Billick calling plays, Minnesota broke the NFL record at the time for most points scored in a season with 556 and also set a franchise record with 41 touchdown passes. This earned Billick the moniker of "offensive guru." He was organized and technologically savvy. Billick was also high on the list of the new Cleveland Browns, who soured on him after he interviewed with the Ravens. Billick was impressed with Baltimore and saw the potential to put together a winning team over the long term.

"Ozzie Newsome is one of the best personnel people in the business," Billick said. "They've got talent, and I was excited by the city of Baltimore, the energy that was there when we [played] there."

Baltimore officially named Billick as the head coach on January 19, 1999. It didn't take long for him to make an impact. The Ravens had a rough start to the season, losing five of their first seven games. Billick benched two quarterbacks, Scott Mitchell and Stoney Case, before deciding to go with Tony Banks, a former second-round pick of the St. Louis Rams from Michigan State. Banks gave Baltimore a spark that season, starting the final 10 games. He threw for 2,136 yards with 17 touchdowns and only eight interceptions.

The season ended with a 20–3 loss on the road to the New England Patriots. The Ravens won four of the final five games and went 8–8—their first non-losing season since the move from Cleveland. Baltimore finished in third place in the AFC Central behind the Jaguars and Titans, and two games ahead of the fourth-place Steelers.

While Billick was disappointed to end the season with a loss, he was confident he had a solid foundation in place to take the next step the following season. Suddenly, there was a bigger buzz surrounding the Ravens. Shortly after the season, the University of Maryland was scheduled to play Duke on a Sunday afternoon, which was a huge game at the time. However, callers on local sports talk radio wanted to discuss the Ravens and how they finally looked like a playoff-caliber team under Billick, who embraced the high expectations.

"It's a group I'm proud of and proud to be a part of," Billick told the media after the Patriots game. "I appreciate everything they did for me in my first year as a head coach. I'm very disappointed to finish it off this way. Hopefully we can learn from this, because this is normally a playoff weekend and that would be about the only value this game would have. You have to win games this time of year. If we didn't learn from it, that would be a real waste."

This modest success was an indicator the team was moving in the right direction. The Ravens were fun to watch. Billick had changed the culture of the team and raised the bar for his fellow coaches, players, and fans. There was a new sense of optimism. With the Cleveland Browns finally back in the NFL, any leftover sense of guilt in Baltimore began to fully dissipate. Cleveland got its justice. And these Ravens belonged to Baltimore and better days were apparently ahead. Nonetheless, no one could have predicted the success of the 2000 season.

The Ravens fan base would have likely been happy just to stay in the thick of the playoff race that season, but they received much, much more. Led by Ray Lewis, the Ravens defense entered that season as one of the fiercest in the league. Baltimore also had two first-round picks for the second time in four years. The Ravens used the fifth overall selection on Tennessee running back Jamal Lewis, whose burly frame was a perfect fit for the physical AFC North. The Ravens took Florida wide receiver Travis Taylor with the 10th overall selection. Baltimore also signed veteran tight end Shannon Sharpe as another weapon on offense and quarterback Trent Dilfer to back up Banks.

However, Baltimore's defense was so stellar that the offense simply had to avoid costly mistakes to win games. The Ravens overcame a five-game drought without scoring a touchdown to finish the season at 12–4, in second place behind the Tennessee Titans. The Ravens defense stated its case during that season as the best unit of all time. Billick made a shrewd move by replacing Banks with Dilfer, who led the team to its first postseason.

The Ravens rolled through the playoffs with victories over Denver, Tennessee, and Oakland. Baltimore then dominated the New York Giants 34–7 in Super Bowl XXXV. It was a masterful coaching job by Billick and an even more impressive showing by the team. The city of Baltimore was in a frenzy, and the Ravens were hailed as local heroes. Downtown became a sea of purple for the team's victory parade.

We'll talk more about this Super Bowl season in a later chapter, but that was the high point of Billick's tenure. The following season, Billick and Newsome decided the team needed a more dynamic quarterback to have any chance at defending its title, even though Dilfer was a consummate leader and was highly respected by his teammates. It was a decision that Billick would eventually regret. Dilfer was replaced by the strong-armed Elvis Grbac, who signed as a free agent following a Pro Bowl year in Kansas City. Grbac inked a five-year, $30 million contract that was to be short-lived. Billick defended the mostly unpopular move.

"Trent will be a free agent, and he has to pursue what is best for him," Billick told the media. "We have to do the same thing. That doesn't mean we can't stay together, but I'm realistic about these things. In today's game, players move on, and that includes quarterbacks."

With much of the defense intact and a new playmaking quarterback, the Ravens were confident they could make a run at a second consecutive Super Bowl. However, the bad omens began at the start of that year's training camp. Running back Jamal Lewis, who was coming off a stellar rookie year, tore his ACL and had to miss the entire season. Baltimore failed to find another running back that could adequately replace him. The ineffective running game would haunt them.

Grbac, however, was the biggest disappointment. He never appeared comfortable in his new environment. Grbac seemed aloof to fans and distant to teammates on the sideline. He was also hampered by the weak running game, so he was forced to throw the ball to move the team down the field. This led to costly mistakes that the team sometimes had trouble overcoming.

Grbac had 15 touchdown passes but 18 interceptions. Baltimore went 0–6 in games Grbac threw two or more interceptions that season. The players and fans lost confidence in him.

Adam Rank of NFL.com graded the Ravens' acquisition of Grbac as the second-worst free-agent quarterback signing in the history of the NFL, behind Miami choosing Daunte Culpepper over Drew Brees.

Elvis Grbac is the quarterback the Ravens signed to replace Dilfer after he led them to a Super Bowl title in 2000. The move—not re-signing Dilfer and bringing in Grbac—was met with mixed emotions. Grbac struggled badly at times and lasted just one year with Baltimore, even though the Ravens did make the playoffs that season.

Ravens fans—and some players—even clamored for backup Randall Cunningham to take over the starting job, but Billick stayed with Grbac throughout the season. He didn't want to shatter what was left of his quarterback's confidence. Baltimore finished the regular season 10–6, three games behind the Steelers. The Ravens managed to beat the Dolphins in the first round of the playoffs before being dismantled by Pittsburgh 27–10 the following week. It was the worst postseason defeat of a defending Super Bowl champion in 18 years. Grbac threw three interceptions in the game. The Steelers knew they would win the game if they could rattle Grbac, which they easily did.

"Grbac doesn't like to get hit, so when we got close to him, we tried to brush him if nothing else, just to let him know we were close by," Pittsburgh outside linebacker Joey Porter said afterward. "When a quarterback isn't confident, that makes for a tough day. We knew he wasn't going to beat us."

The disappointing 2001 season was costly on several levels. The team was a projected $20.5 million over the salary cap, forcing a complete overhaul of the roster that included the release of 11 starters. Some of those key playmakers were Sam Adams, Rob Burnett, Sam Gash, Qadry Ismail, Tony Siragusa, Sharpe, Larry Webster, and Rod Woodson.

Grbac, however, declined to restructure his contract to provide some added relief. As a result, he was released in March and later decided to retire. Now Baltimore was forced to find a fourth starting quarterback in as many seasons, which was a recipe for upcoming disaster. The shimmer of the recent Super Bowl victory wasn't as bright, and Billick was facing an uphill battle as the head coach just one year removed from succeeding at the highest level.

"We're disappointed for us and for Elvis," Billick said in a postseason news conference to announce the release of Grbac. "We thought a new contract would not only give us obvious help with our salary cap, but benefit Elvis too. We were looking forward to facing the challenges of next season, when we believed he would play at a higher level for us."

Billick turned to Chris Redman to lead the team at quarterback for the 2002 season. Redman, like the great and revered John Unitas, attended Louisville and publicly paid homage to the former Baltimore Colts great. He split time with journeyman Jeff Blake that season, but neither was overly effective. Billick never backed down from adversity and was prepared to meet this challenge head-on. However, the season neither started nor ended well. Baltimore lost its first two games and scored just seven points over that stretch. Adding to the problems, linebacker Ray Lewis suffered a shoulder injury October 6 in Cleveland and played in just five games.

Baltimore finished 7–9 in the first season under the realigned AFC North—the worst campaign under Billick. The team, though, was prepared for that rough patch because of the loss of so many veterans, and now it was time to build another winner. Besides, the 2002 season wasn't a total loss. The team drafted safety Ed Reed from the University of Miami in the first round. He had already showed flashes of his big-time playmaking ability in his rookie season. Reed was one of several young players on the roster that Billick was confident could help the team get back on track.

The premonition proved to be accurate, as Baltimore bounced back the following season with yet another new starting quarterback, Kyle Boller, a first-round pick (19th overall) from California. Boller started the first nine games, going 5–4 before suffering a thigh injury. This opened the door for Anthony Wright to take over the starting role, and he did a solid job managing the game. The Ravens went 10–6 and won the AFC North. But they were bounced from the playoffs with a 20–17 loss to the Tennessee Titans in the Wild Card round.

Still, it was a memorable season. Not only did the Ravens win their first division title, they had a relatively young roster that was capable of making playoff runs over the next couple of years. One of the biggest highlights was running back Jamal Lewis, who set the NFL record for most rushing yards in a single game when he scampered for 295 yards on September 14, 2003, against the Cleveland Browns.

Billick, however, was facing some criticism for a floundering offense, especially with the passing game. This was becoming a concerning trend over his head coaching career. During Billick's five seasons, the Ravens' offense was ranked in the bottom half of the league in all but one of those years. The offense also was never ranked higher than 14th overall. Teams could simply stack the box to stop Jamal Lewis because they were confident the Ravens quarterbacks could not beat them. Lewis did his best to manage that role, but Baltimore simply needed an improved passing game to help him.

The brunt of the blame was directed at offensive coordinator Matt Cavanaugh. After the loss to the Titans in the playoffs, the fans were clamoring for Billick to hire a more dynamic coach to run the offense. Billick, however, remained loyal to his staff. "In my opinion, those that want to focus on that [passing ranking] show their lack of understanding of this game and their lack of appreciation for how this season unfolded," Billick said at his post-season press conference. "Go back to the early years of the franchise when they were up and down the field and had yards galore. Yet we've scored more points [this season] than at any time." The defiant attitude did not sit well with fans...or ownership.

Billick was confident he finally had the team's franchise quarterback in Boller. Baltimore traded a second-round pick in 2003 and its first-round selection in 2004 to the Patriots to move up and acquire him. It cost the Ravens a valuable player because New England was able to grab nose guard Vince Wilfork with that first-round pick the following year. Wilfork was an All-Pro player for the Patriots and was a force for them over 11 seasons.

Still, Billick was prepared to move forward with Boller at quarterback with Wright as a capable backup. Boller certainly had enough arm strength to get the ball downfield. However, there were numerous questions surrounding his accuracy and overall decision-making. Boller also appeared prone to costly turnovers, which was the one area Baltimore needed to avoid. The team still had a stout defense and there was no reason to put them under added pressure with a short field. Still, Billick was convinced Boller was the long-term answer.

"We think we have our quarterback of the future in both Kyle Boller and Anthony Wright," Billick said. "We can feel very good about that and the litany of quarterbacks we've gone through and the success we've had with it. I think it's a testimony to our ability to adapt to the talent that we've had."

The following year, though, the team had another inconsistent season. Baltimore won five out of six midseason to improve to 7–3.

However, the Ravens then lost four of their final six games and finished 7–9. The team ended up in second place behind the 15–1 Steelers, whose only loss was a 30–13 setback against Baltimore in Week 2. The Ravens' season was further marred by a suspension of Jamal Lewis after he pleaded guilty to a drug offense. Baltimore was forced to overcome injuries to six players who had previously made the Pro Bowl. Neither Billick nor his players were able to overcome that adversity.

Boller started all 16 games and had a career-high 13 touchdowns with 11 interceptions. He also completed 258-of-464 (55.6 percent) for 2,559 yards. However, he did not exactly instill further confidence in the fan base. Furthermore, Billick was still facing questions about the future of Cavanaugh and fixing the sputtering offense, which was still a source of frustration. In return, Billick was still defensive about the topic. When asked about the future of Cavanaugh after the final game in Miami, Billick snapped, "Obviously, if you're not interested in talking about this game, my part of the news conference is over." He then left the podium in the interview room, which did not sit well with the media.

This was also the year that Steve Bisciotti took over full ownership from Modell, and Billick appeared to be officially on the hot seat. Bisciotti was a self-made millionaire who liked to see positive results. It was sometimes difficult to determine which way Billick and the rest of the franchise were trending. Still, Billick was 56–40 over six seasons—a record most NFL teams would embrace.

Nonetheless, Billick finally listened to the outcry for changes on offense. Cavanaugh was replaced by Jim Fassel as the coordinator. While this move was supposed to help improve performance, it began another era of turmoil. Baltimore also added a pair of talented receivers—veteran Derrick Mason and rookie Mark Clayton—in the offseason to provide a further spark. Boller remained the starter, and the Ravens were optimistic he was ready to take the next step in his career. However, he missed eight games because of a toe injury suffered in the season opener. There were some cheers at M&T Bank Stadium when Boller went down with the injury, prompting some outrage from the players and fan base about the reaction.

"I love the fans of Baltimore, but that was a little bit classless," defensive end Tony Weaver said after the game. "Kyle is our guy. He is our quarterback, and we are going to stand by him." Despite the injury, Boller completed 171-of-293 passes for 1,799 yards with 11 touchdowns but 12 interceptions. This erratic play exhausted the patience of the fans.

Baltimore also had another disappointing season, finishing 6–10 and in third place in the AFC North. The Ravens missed the playoffs for the second consecutive season, prompting another offseason of massive change. The biggest upgrade was at quarterback, when the Ravens signed veteran Steve McNair, who immediately created a buzz around the team. Despite the down year, the addition of McNair created Super Bowl rumblings heading into the 2005 opener and the Ravens appeared ready to meet those expectations.

The season, however, was full of more controversy. As the offense continued to struggle even with McNair at quarterback, Billick made another bold move. On October 17, 2006, he fired Fassel as the offensive coordinator during the bye week. Under Fassel's system, McNair had a 64.1 quarterback rating with five touchdown passes and seven interceptions.

Despite the struggles, Baltimore had a winning record at the time. Sensing that an urgent move needed to be made, Billick took on the responsibilities of offensive coordinator and called the plays during games.

"Clearly, in order for us to expand on our 4–2 start, we have to have more offensive productivity," Billick said at a news conference to announce the change. "It was my opinion going forward, in order to bring about the level of production that we need offensively to get where we want to go, that I needed to step back in on a day-to-day basis."

The move appeared to spark the team. The Ravens won nine of the final 10 games but were only 17th in the league in total offense. The defense, however, was ranked first in the league and carried the team to 13–3 finish, which set the franchise record for wins in a season. Baltimore also ran away with the AFC North title.

There was unmitigated excitement with potential home-field advantage throughout the postseason. Baltimore was the second seed behind the 14–2 San Diego Chargers. But the year ended with a thud as the Ravens were bounced from the AFC Divisional round of the playoffs with a disheartening 15–6 loss to the hated Indianapolis Colts at home.

Once again, the offense was the culprit. Baltimore's defense came up big and contained the Colts' All-Pro quarterback Peyton Manning. Indianapolis did not manage a touchdown and got all of its points off five Adam Vinatieri field goals. The Ravens offense, however, could not manage a touchdown and committed four costly turnovers. The setback was especially disappointing because it came against the Colts. Many fans in Baltimore were still angry about the move to Indianapolis and a win over the Colts could have gone a long way in exorcising those demons.

"This football team is as disappointed as our fans are, which is matched tenfold by the players," a dejected Billick said after the game. "[The fans] were deserving of better than that, but it just wasn't going to happen and we will move forward now."

Moving forward was a lot more difficult than Billick could have predicted, especially with a quarterback heading into the back end of his career. Billick also could not have fathomed that the 2007 season would be the final one of his career. Baltimore was hoping to take the next step after managing 13 wins the prior year. Billick named Rick Neuheisel as the offensive coordinator so Billick could focus more on the big picture. The result was a 5–11 finish—Billick's worst mark as the head coach. The poor record, however, was just the beginning of the problems.

The team lacked energy and endured a nine-game losing streak in the final stretch of the season. This included a 26–20 overtime loss to the previously winless Miami Dolphins. The Ravens had a chance to win the game when they moved the ball to the 1-foot line with eight seconds left. Billick decided to settle for a game-tying field goal to send the game into overtime, rather than go for a win against a team that was playing for nothing more than pride. After converting the game-tying field goal, the usually reliable Matt Stover missed a 44-yard attempt on the first possession of the extra period, opening the door for Miami to win the game. It was an inexplicable loss that left Bisciotti seething and might have sealed Billick's fate.

Less than 24 hours after Baltimore managed an uplifting 27–21 victory over the Pittsburgh Steelers in the season finale on

December 30, 2007, Billick and his entire coaching staff, including defensive coordinator Rex Ryan, were fired. Bisciotti made the decision after a meeting with Ravens president Dick Cass and Newsome. Since Bisciotti had taken over the team in 2004, Billick was just 33–33 as the head coach.

"I believed that it was time for a change. I believed that we had the nucleus of a team that can get back to the Super Bowl, and we felt that in the next five years we had a better chance with a new coach than leaving Brian in that position," Bisciotti said at a news conference to announce his decision. "It's a gut feeling. I have one job here, and that's to have a leader that I think gives us the best chance We have been losing more than winning lately."

Billick still had three years remaining on a contract that paid him $5 million per season. Nonetheless, Bisciotti decided to make the bold move. After nine seasons, Billick's voice simply no longer resonated with the veteran players. "Sometimes the message can get repetitive after awhile," Ogden said. With a Super Bowl victory on his resume, it initially appeared that Billick would have little trouble landing another head coaching gig.

Still, one of the biggest frustrations with Billick was not being able to put together an effective offense to complement the team's dominant defense. Many of the players were convinced the Ravens could have won multiple championships if they had been able to strike a better balance. In Billick's final season, the Ravens were ranked 22nd in total offense but sixth in defense. He was never able to recapture any of the success he enjoyed in Minnesota.

"Whenever you have a bad year, somebody's got to be held accountable," Ogden said. "By no means is it ever [the fault of just] the head coach, but they take the fall unfortunately. Things happened to us this year, but it's just the unfortunate nature of the way this business is. Produce or you're not going to be here."

Overall, though, Billick went 85–67 over his nine seasons. He was 5–3 in the postseason. During the Super Bowl run in 2000, Baltimore went five games without scoring an offensive touchdown. However, the team managed to win two of those games because of its suffocating defense. Ultimately, Billick struggled because he could never find a true franchise quarterback that could help carry the team. The decision to draft Boller was particularly damaging. The quarterback's struggles over his five seasons in Baltimore corresponded with some of the worst years of Billick's tenure.

This was especially costly for Billick's future as a head coach in the NFL. After being fired by the Ravens, Billick never landed another job as other teams appeared to sour on him. There was a sense his time had passed as a head coach. Furthermore, Billick was not willing to go back to being a coordinator to show his offense could work and regain some of his reputation. The longer he stayed out of the coaching ranks, the move his opportunities dwindled. Teams looked for other up-and-coming coordinators that were ready to take the next step into head coaching positions as opposed to retreads.

However, Billick is an exceptional orator and is highly knowledgeable about the game. These skills led to a successful broadcasting career and work as a public speaker. Nonetheless, he often thinks back about how his career might have been different if he had just landed an exceptional playmaker behind center. Who knows? He might have won multiple championships, like his mentor Bill Walsh.

"I am living proof that if you miss on a first-round quarterback, as I did with Kyle Boller, you end up broadcasting games and writing about the NFL instead of coaching," Billick said years after giving up on another coaching gig.

STAN'S SIDEBAR

ON BRIAN BILLICK

Brian Billick is very easy to work with. Great guy; really good coach. I used to disagree with him on methodology, but I couldn't argue when he was being so successful, you know? But eventually, I think the problem was they'd have a good year, a bad year, a good year, a bad year. You've got to keep getting better, so after that good year, I don't think the players would be quite as intense going into the next year, and then they'd have a bad year, and they'd be more intense going into the next year.

Billick was easy to interview at halftime because he wasn't nearly as emotional. He's very laissez-faire, you know? This is the way things are. "It is what it is" is one of his favorite sayings. But he's a heck of a football coach. I'm really surprised he never got another job. I think he priced himself out of the market. He had made so much money that if he was going back into that pressure cooker, he'd have to be paid well, because he was doing all these different things on TV and making pretty good money doing that. You see a lot of these coaches now, like Jon Gruden, and life's a lot easier not being a coach.

In the NFL, your job's at stake every year. Every game your job's at stake, basically. And you have all these assistant coaches and their families who are depending on you to win; you've got all the players. As a player I saw what happens when you don't win. Even when you win, players are cut. It's a very cutthroat business. It doesn't matter if you have eight kids in school. You're cut and you're gone. Nothing else is taken into consideration. There's no mercy. There's nothing like that. It's just a cutthroat business with a lot of injuries and a lot of tough time down. It's a very short career on average. It's not all fun and games. Billick was organized. He knew what he wanted. He was able to use his methodology early to get the players to buy into what they needed to do. Then they started to take more and more inches, then more miles, and it got out of control. Once you lose control, it's almost impossible to get it back as a coach. It's gone.

You have to change to get it back under control, and when you change, people know that's not you. It's like the phony rah-rah guy, you know? You can't be a phony out there. Joe Flacco can't go out there and jump and holler and run around, because that's not him, and players would see through that right away. They know who he is. You can't invent that stuff. You've got to be who you are, and that's why once you lose it, you can't get it back. You have to go someplace else and start over.

CHAPTER 5
HARBS

John Harbaugh took over as the team's head coach in 2008 and quickly found success. He repeatedly led the team to the playoffs and a Super Bowl title in 2012, beating the San Francisco 49ers, coached by his brother, Jim, in a wild game. The Ravens have struggled a bit since then, and the 2017 season could be a big one for Harbaugh. Many wonder if he's on the hot seat.

The Ravens were determined to find the best coach to lead them back to another Super Bowl. Bisciotti and the front office initially had their sights on Dallas Cowboys offensive coordinator Jason Garrett, who could potentially put together the type of attack the Ravens sorely lacked. The Cowboys did not want to lose Garrett, and owner Jerry Jones offered Garrett a promotion to assistant head coach. After visiting Baltimore, Garrett decided to take Jones' offer and stay in Dallas, where he would eventually take over the top coaching job in 2010. Baltimore also considered New York Jets offensive coordinator Brian Schottenheimer, who interviewed for the position but was ultimately passed over.

Bisciotti thought outside the box when he brought in Philadelphia Eagles secondary coach John Harbaugh for an interview. Generally, head coaching opportunities go to high-profile offensive and defensive coordinators. Harbaugh, however, was different. He was a football guy through-and-through. His father, Jack Harbaugh, was a football coach for more than four decades and won the 2002 Division I-AA national championship at the helm of Western Kentucky. John Harbaugh's brother, Jim, was the starting quarterback at Michigan and even played for the Ravens in 2008. So the entire Harbaugh family had the pedigree to lead a football team.

After a mediocre playing career at Miami University in Ohio, John Harbaugh had a meteoric rise up the coaching ladder. He spent time coaching at his alma mater, Western Michigan, as well as Pittsburgh, Morehead State, and Cincinnati. That experience led to an assistant coaching job with the Philadelphia Eagles in 1998. His meticulous approach to the game earned him NFL Special Teams Coach of the Year honors in 2001. Harbaugh later shifted to secondary coach, where he worked under defensive coordinator Jim Johnson.

The Ravens were impressed by Harbaugh's coaching acumen after he interviewed with the team on January 8, 2006. Harbaugh was organized, energetic, and had a clear plan to get the franchise back on track. Most of the Ravens fan base, however, had never heard of him prior to his interview with the team. Nonetheless, Harbaugh showed the brass that he was the best man for the job and officially became the third head coach in the history of the Ravens on January 19, 2008. Harbaugh had also been a finalist for the head job at UCLA the prior month and was considered for the top coaching position for the Miami Dolphins in 2007. Baltimore, however, appeared to be the best fit.

"Do I like a guy that has to earn his resume? Yeah," Bisciotti said at the introductory press conference. "I kind of made a living on hiring people with thin resumes, and it's worked out pretty well for me in the last 25 years. I think that works to John's advantage. I said three weeks ago you have to take chances to be successful. You have to be willing to do things that the masses wouldn't do, or I don't think you will be able to separate yourself from the masses. Is it a little bit more of a perceived chance? Yeah, but the time we spent with John Harbaugh gave me a comfort level that we hired the right guy. You go with your instincts, and I have pretty good instincts."

Harbaugh displayed the same type of charisma and energy he showed in his interviews at his introductory press conference. He was focused and confident. Bisciotti appeared delighted that he had found the best candidate to lead the team after Billick had faltered in his final years. Harbaugh dismissed any notion that he was even remotely peeved that he was the apparent second choice behind Garrett. Instead, he was ready to embrace an opportunity that was the culmination of a life spent around football.

"As far as being perceived as the second choice, that's irrelevant to me," Harbaugh said. "I never thought about it in those terms, never would. It doesn't matter. It's an opportunity to go forward. I know they looked at six great coaches here, any one of whom could have done a great job. I feel fortunate to be the one that's going to get the shot."

The Eagles organization also expressed confidence that the Ravens picked the correct coach to lead their team. There was no ambivalence about Harbaugh taking the promotion. He earned the opportunity with all of his hard work in Philadelphia. Besides, he was going to a team outside the conference, so they would only have to deal with him once every four years when the NFC East and the AFC North played one another under the cyclical NFL schedule.

"I couldn't be happier for John and his entire family," said Andy Reid, the Eagles head coach at the time. "He has worked very hard to become a head coach in the National Football League. I know how much this means to him. He is very deserving of this opportunity and we will miss him in Philadelphia. John is a good friend, a great coach, and he has played a vital role in the success we have shared here. I wish him all the best in Baltimore."

Harbaugh wasted little time putting his stamp on the team and laying the groundwork for long-term success. The goal was to establish a perennial playoff contender, rather than having a team that drifts up and down the standings year after year. Harbaugh quickly went to work, adding the necessary pieces to solve that puzzle.

Baltimore made its first strike in the 2008 NFL Draft, which set in motion that successful strategy. With the 18th overall selection, the Ravens were confident they had found their franchise quarterback in Joe Flacco. The strong-armed Flacco became the highest-drafted player out of the University of Delaware, which also produced another stellar quarterback in Rich Gannon. In the second round, Baltimore got its coveted running back with Ray Rice, who was a Heisman Trophy Award candidate and set a program record for rushing touchdowns at Rutgers.

It was a bounce-back year for the Ravens, who also immediately injected excitement into the local fan base. Baltimore went 11–5 and finished in second place behind the Steelers. The Ravens then topped the Miami Dolphins in the Wild Card game before upsetting top-seeded Tennessee in the AFC divisional round. This earned them a spot in the AFC championship game. However, the impressive postseason run ended there with a 23–14 loss to archrival Pittsburgh.

"I want to say how proud I am of our football team," Harbaugh said after the game. "I thought our guys, throughout the course of this season and the course of this game, demonstrated who they are as men and what they're all about. I couldn't be more proud to stand with them in victory and today in defeat."

Despite that heartbreaking loss, Harbaugh's first season was a rousing success by any standard. Harbaugh tied the NFL record by taking over a sub-.500 team the previous season and leading it to an 11–5 record. With 13 total victories, including the two wins in the playoffs, Harbaugh set the NFL record for the most wins ever by a rookie head coach starting a rookie quarterback.

The defense also did not lose a beat under Harbaugh and was ranked No. 2 in the NFL, allowing 261.1 yards per game.

The defense ranked No. 3 in points allowed per game (15.3) and had a league-best 26 interceptions, five of which were returned for touchdowns. Safety Ed Reed continued his potential Hall-of-Fame career and tied his career high with nine interceptions, also best in the league.

Five players earned Pro Bowl honors: linebacker Ray Lewis, Reed, safety Brendon Ayanbadejo, linebacker Terrell Suggs, and fullback Le'Ron McClain. Flacco lived up to the expectations as the team's first-round draft pick and was the first rookie quarterback in NFL history to win two playoff games. Over the 19 games that season (regular season and playoffs), Flacco threw for 3,408 yards with 15 touchdowns and 15 interceptions and was named the Diet Pepsi Rookie of the Year.

Most of that momentum carried into 2009. Baltimore did suffer a blow when defensive coordinator Rex Ryan took the head coaching job for the New York Jets. The Ravens also lost two key defensive players in linebacker Bart Scott and safety Jim Leonhard. While the Ravens went 9–7, they still earned a spot in the playoffs. Baltimore stunned New England in the Wild Card round with a 33–14 victory. On the Ravens' first possession, Rice ran for an 83-yard touchdown before most of the Patriots fans even found their seats. However, the Colts once again knocked Baltimore out of the postseason during the next game with a 20–3 victory. Flacco was just 20-of-38 for 189 yards and two interceptions. Adding to the disappointment was the fact that this was Indianapolis' eighth consecutive win over Baltimore, including two heart-wrenching setbacks in the playoffs.

Overall, though, it was a successful season for Harbaugh and his staff thanks to earning a second consecutive trip to the playoffs. The victory over New England was especially sweet after losing to the Patriots in Week 4. Harbaugh, however, had raised the bar, and he made it clear that anything short of hoisting the Lombardi Trophy at the end of the season was disappointing.

"Obviously, we're not where we want to be right now," Harbaugh said. "We want to [get to] the point where we can win the divisional playoff game, we can win the AFC championship game, and we can win the Super Bowl. We tried like crazy to be good, enough to do that. We're not good enough yet. We have to find a way to make our team better."

Harbaugh continued to keep the team moving in the right direction. The usually dependable Newsome and the draft department, however, made one of the biggest mistakes of their time with the team when Newsome drafted the troubled and oft-injured linebacker Sergio Kindle from Texas in the second round of the NFL Draft. The troubles for Kindle started almost immediately. He fell down a flight of steps at his home and suffered a fractured skull just prior to training camp. That ended his rookie season and then, ostensibly, his career. Kindle never became an impact player and was eventually released by the team in 2013. It was a rare stumble by the Ravens' usually reliable scouts. Despite his troubled tenure with the team, however, Kindle valued his short time in Baltimore.

"I really feel like this organization is so much more than football, you know?" he told reporters after he was released from the practice squad. "I can honestly say they really care about players, and that goes from the head man all the way down."

The defense had the depth to absorb that loss in 2010, and Harbaugh led the Ravens to another successful season. Baltimore won six of its final seven games and finished 12–4, good for second place in the AFC North behind the Pittsburgh Steelers on the tiebreaker. The Ravens then dominated Kansas City 30–7 at Arrowhead Stadium in the first round of the playoffs. The defense forced five turnovers and Flacco threw a pair of touchdown passes without a turnover. It was the third consecutive year Harbaugh and the Ravens won a Wild Card game. Baltimore also improved to 7–3 all time on the road in the postseason.

This set up another postseason showdown in Pittsburgh. The teams split their regular season games, with both teams winning on the road. This latest matchup would prove to be yet another heated affair, which set the tone for what was considered one of the best rivalries in the entire NFL. The Ravens led 21–7 at halftime before collapsing. Baltimore had three turnovers in the third quarter to let Pittsburgh back in the game. Running back Rashard Mendenhall scored on a two-yard touchdown with 1:33 left in the fourth quarter to give the Steelers a 31–24 victory. It was a stunning, bitter loss to a divisional rival that just seemed to have the Ravens' number in big games. Harbaugh, however, showed his leadership skills by remaining stoic in the face of disappointment.

"All you can do in life is to take a shot at being great," Harbaugh said after the game. "That's all you can do. Our guys did that. We just weren't great enough today. We'll be back." He later added, "We've got a lot of work to do. We'll have to build our team the best way we can to be able to be great enough to win these kinds of games."

The Ravens faced more challenges in the offseason with almost half of their starters poised to hit the free agent market, including defensive tackle Haloti Ngata and offensive tackle Marshal Yanda. Harbaugh would successfully navigate the troubled waters once again when Ngata left for Detroit, but Yanda stayed in Baltimore and was the anchor of the offensive line.

Baltimore had become a model franchise under Harbaugh. The Ravens consistently stayed competitive and fought for division titles each year with him at the helm. The 2011 season was no different, as Baltimore rolled through the regular season at 12–4 and won its third AFC North title in franchise history by taking the tiebreaker with the Steelers. The Ravens went an impressive 6–0 in the division.

This led to a home playoff game in the divisional round against the Houston Texans. The Ravens defense led the way again, forcing three turnovers in the 20–13 victory. Flacco threw a pair of touchdown passes, continuing to come up big in the postseason. While the Ravens were a bit short on style points, they knew how to win. They would need that moxie with another playoff game looming in New England—a place that didn't intimidate them as much as other teams. "There's a right way to do things, there's a wrong way to do things, and there's the Ravens way to do things," Suggs said after the Texans game.

Baltimore, however, suffered one of its most crushing defeats in franchise history in that AFC Championship game against the Patriots. The Ravens controlled the run of play most of the way and led 20–16 heading into the final quarter. But Patriots quarterback Tom Brady, who was held without a touchdown pass, finally gave his team the lead with a one-yard score.

The Ravens fought back and put themselves in position to go ahead again in the final minutes of the game, but calamity struck. First, Lee Evans dropped a potential 14-yard touchdown pass from Flacco. The ball was right in Evans' hands before it was knocked away by Patriots defensive back Sterling Moore. It is a moment that still irks Ravens fans.

"Honestly, the most disappointing part of all this [is] that I feel personally that I let everybody down," Evans said after the game. "This is the greatest team that I've been on, and I feel like I let everybody down. Yeah, it's on my shoulders. I think Ray [Lewis] gave a good message coming in here. It's hard to sit here and accept how and why things happened, but it's the reality of it. It's as tough as it gets."

Despite the dropped pass by Evans, the Ravens were still in position to tie the game. They just needed a 32-yard field goal from the sure-footed Billy Cundiff. The clock was racing down and Baltimore had to hurry to get the snap off. In the frantic movement, the ball was snapped and Cundiff's kick sailed wide left. The Ravens lost 23–20 and the Patriots were headed back to the Super Bowl. The Baltimore players stood stunned on the sidelines. Cundiff wasn't sure how to react. It was a kick he had easily made hundreds of times.

To his credit, Cundiff faced the media after the game and took full responsibility for the miss. "First and foremost is to stand up and face the music and move on," he told reporters after the game. However, it was the last kick Cundiff would ever attempt for Baltimore. His name would go down in infamy. Yet Harbaugh wasn't about to lay the blame at any one player for the disappointment.

"It's two great football teams—two gladiators, I guess, just kind of going at each other at the end, and I'm proud of our guys," Harbaugh said. "You know, we've got 53 guys—mighty men, as we like to call them—and they fought, and we came up a little bit short, as 53. You know, 53 win and 53 lose."

Despite that heartbreaking loss, Harbaugh and the players vowed to get better and bounce back the following season. The reality, though, is the window of opportunity was closing for some key veterans who gave their heart and soul to the franchise, especially Ray Lewis and Ed Reed, both of whom were sure future Hall of Famers. Baltimore had the pieces in place to make that elusive Super Bowl run. The team just needed to make a few more plays. Flacco had a big enough arm to lead the offense and the defense was still dominant. "We have to keep moving and keep building and remember this taste no matter how many times you go through it," Lewis said. "Because when you finally get it, you appreciate it more."

Lewis had already won a Super Bowl in 2000. Now, at the end of his career, he wanted nothing more than to win another and ride off into the sunset. Reed had been one of the league's most electrifying playmakers since he was drafted by the Ravens in the 2002 NFL Draft. However, he had to yet to play in the league's biggest game—the Super Bowl. He was determined to get there with the Ravens.

The hard work and dedication finally paid off in 2012 even though few people predicted that type of success. Baltimore had the formula to make a magical run to the title game after falling just short over the past two years. The team was able to accomplish that feat even after it appeared to have taken a step back from the previous year. Just like Suggs preached, the Ravens never do anything easy.

Baltimore lost four of its final five games of the 2012 season to finish 10–6, yet they still managed to win the AFC North with the tiebreaker over the Bengals. Baltimore had captured the divisional title in back-to-back years for the first time in franchise history. Nonetheless, Baltimore wasn't exactly carrying any momentum into the postseason. They also had to face their old nemesis, the Colts, in the Wild Card round of the playoffs. Fans still remembered that painful loss against Indianapolis in the 2007 postseason. This was a game the Ravens just had to win. The Colts coach Chuck Pagano had been the Ravens defensive coordinator in 2011, so he had some familiarity with the team.

The game took on even more significance because it was potentially the last home game for Lewis, who had just announced his plans to retire after 17 years in the league. There was certainly no way Lewis was going to take a loss in his final home game, especially against the hated Colts. But one thing was for sure—he was at peace with his decision to call it quits.

"Everything that starts has an end. It's just life. And for me, today I told my team that this will be my last ride," Lewis said after meeting with the team midweek before the playoff game. "I told them I just felt so much peace at where I am with my decision because of everything I've done in this league. I've done it, man."

The announcement caught some of Lewis' teammates off guard. They knew 17 years is a long time to play in the NFL. However, Lewis was such a fixture with the franchise from Day 1, it was going to be odd without him around. "I can't picture Baltimore without him," running back Ray Rice said. "Baltimore is Ray Lewis." Harbaugh was about to lose one of his most vocal leaders in the locker room. But for now, the focus was solely on beating the Colts.

Baltimore responded by dominating the Colts 24–9, finally exorcising some of the demons from the move in 1984. Veteran

Anquan Boldin set a franchise record with 145 receiving yards. But it was Lewis who basked in the glow. He finished the game with 13 tackles and lined up at fullback for the final snap. Lewis celebrated the victory by doing his trademark pregame dance before taking one final victory lap.

"My only focus was to come in and get my team a win. Nothing else was planned," he said after the game. "It's one of those things, when you recap it all and try to say what is one of your greatest moments."

The Ravens then advanced to the AFC Championship with a stunning 38–35 victory over the Denver Broncos in what became known as the Mile High Miracle when Flacco threw a game-tying 70-yard pass to Jacoby Jones in the final minute. Justin Tucker would boot the winning field goal in overtime.

The Ravens got another monkey off their back by dominating the host Patriots 28–13 in the AFC Championship. That set up the Ravens' second Super Bowl against the 49ers with perhaps one of the best storylines in the history of the game: brother-against-brother with John Harbaugh vs. Jim Harbaugh. The younger Harbaugh and the Ravens would prevail 34–31 in a bizarre game that featured a power outage while Baltimore was leading 28–6.

By winning the Super Bowl, Harbaugh will always be immortalized in Baltimore sports history. The goal, however, is to win on a consistent basis. As Lewis and Reed eventually left the franchise, the Ravens have struggled to find consistent playmakers. Harbaugh and the franchise had to navigate more troubled waters with the Ray Rice domestic abuse case in 2014 that ended the running back's career and changed the way the Ravens drafted players.

Through it all, though, Harbaugh has remained the leader. He has stood up to adversity and promised to keep the team moving in the right direction. Harbaugh was especially criticized after an injury-marred season in 2015 led to a 5–11 finish—the worst mark in Harbaugh's career. The team bounced back in 2016 by going 8–8, but it was not enough to make the postseason. Harbaugh also parted ways with another offensive coordinator, Marc Trestman. Suddenly there were doubts about Harbaugh's future with the team. Harbaugh said he never gave a second thought to his job status, despite the disappointing finish. After the 2016 season, Ravens owner Steve Bisciotti gave some insight into his philosophy for running the team and retaining quality people.

"I didn't get where I [am] by just firing people," Bisciotti said. "I think it's a bad model, especially in this business. I don't have as much to fall back on except to then say, 'Trust me, this is the right way to run a business.' That's not good enough for probably a quarter of our fans. That's fine with me. I'll be more than happy to take the blame for that."

Still, Bisciotti acknowledged the team needed to play better, and everyone was accountable. The owner was confident the best people were in place to make a run at a third Super Bowl. Just like in 2012, the Ravens needed to make a few extra plays and have the ball bounce their way a few more times.

"I want my fans to know that I think John can coach better," Bisciotti said. "I think Ozzie and Eric [DeCosta, assistant general manager] can draft better. I think Joe can play better. If all of them do it—and I think they're capable and determined to be better—then I think next year we're sitting here with a playoff-caliber team. I really believe that. If you get improvement from quality people, I believe they can collectively bring this team back to prominence."

Despite the ups and downs, Harbaugh still appears to be the right man to lead the Ravens.

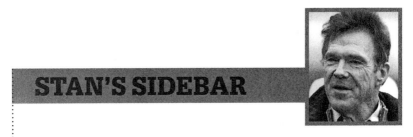

STAN'S SIDEBAR

ON JOHN HARBAUGH

John is a very intense, very old-school football coach who believes in the way I was brought up—he comes from the same tree that I come from, Woody Hayes to Bo Schembechler to his father—and that's having a great defense, having great special teams, making big plays on offense, and having discipline. He always wants a disciplined football team, and he has a certain way he wants things done, and he's going to make sure it gets done that way. He's smart enough to know how to massage that, especially when he came in here after Brian Billick, who had probably let things get a little too far as far as the players and the way they wanted to do things. John was going to let the players have input but not control, because he knows what he wants on a football team. And that goes back to that chant that he has—"the team, the team, the team." The team's always more important than the individual. If it's good for the team, it's good for you. When my son was at Ohio State, when they moved him from linebacker to tight end and fullback, he called me, and I said, "It goes back to what I've always told you. If it's good for the team, it's good for you, so you need to do that." And John is the same way with his players. If it's good for the team, then it's good for you individually. It was hard at first. It's human nature that if you give people an inch, they'll take a mile. That's just the way my experience has been with players. You always have to have limits, you have to have boundaries. A players' coach is good at the beginning, because he usually takes over from a guy who had a lot of discipline. The players enjoy that, and they rally around that, but then human nature takes over, and they go further and further and further and take advantage of it and they become less disciplined and less organized and less of a team.

So John had to convince guys like Ed Reed and Ray Lewis. I don't know if Ed Reed was ever convinced until they won the Super Bowl. Then he finally went up to John and said, "I see what you mean, you know, what it takes to be a champion." That's discipline, that's organization, that's structure—all those things it takes to have a successful franchise, and that's all the way from the owner down to the general manager down to the equipment manager. John is like that. He's going to be involved in all phases of it and let people know what they need to do. He's going to pat them on the back when they do it and tell them what they need to do when they don't.

The infamous 2012 meeting between the players was notable for how John handled it. It has been described as a mutiny. I think that's an exaggeration of the term. It was between Bernard Pollard and Ed Reed and a few other guys who had been in different systems where they didn't practice as hard. John came up from the same system I did. I played 13 years and never had a day in summer camps where we didn't have two practices, both of them in pads. He understands what's good now from a safety standpoint, but he also understands what it takes to be a tough, disciplined football team. You just can't go out there in shorts all the time, because you don't play football in shorts.

67

There's another old saying: "If you're going to play in the North Atlantic, you've got to practice in the North Atlantic." It's a General Patton statement that Woody Hayes picked up and Bo Schembechler handed down. You have to practice the way you're going to play. John believes in that. The players weren't buying into it. They were saying their bodies needed to rest, and they needed all this stuff, but winning overcomes that. Success overcomes that. It's like coaching a high school team. If you want to teach a kid to be a man, you'd better win, because he won't listen to you if you don't. If you're losing, he's going to say, "What do you know? You can't even help us win football games." You want to teach him about how to treat women and how to do his schoolwork and all those other things—all the lessons it takes to grow up. You'd better be successful on the field, and they'll listen to what you have to say. I think it's the same thing in the pros, because football players are just big kids.

The saying goes, "Men grow older but they never grow up." Anybody who has gone back to a high school reunion and realizes how they start to act when they're around their old friends realizes that. But John had to get the players to buy into that. The key was Ray buying into that, because Ray's a little old-school himself, and he believes in discipline, and he believes in hard work and those things. While Ray may not have jumped on board right away, I think he did get on board, and I think between him and John, that's what led that whole thing, because Ray was hurt too, that whole season. I think that led to the whole reorganization of the troops after that meeting. They just thought they were practicing too hard.

They wanted John to cut back and wanted him to give them more time off, not as many meetings, all those different things. You win the game during the week. If you don't prepare well, you're not going to win unless you're so vastly better than the other team, and even then, if you don't prepare well, that's why you get upsets all the time. Teams start to relax a little bit. Oh, these guys are 0–12, and we've got to play them this week. You have to have that discipline. You have to continue to prepare. You've got to get better every week.

Another old axiom—"If you're not getting better, you're getting worse." You never stay the same. So you better be getting better, or you're going backward. Each week, you've got to get better as a team, and I think that's what they finally bought into.

I would always go back to Coach Harbaugh during the week and talk about the game. The first moment I had with him was during his first year. We were playing Tennessee. There were a bunch of penalties in the first half, and I had somebody say something in my ear: "Ask him about the penalties." And I thought it was a good idea, so I asked him about the penalties, and it was not the right idea. I said, "They're really getting physical out here with all these penalties." He said, *"Yes. They. Are."* He was very upset about it. As you remember, the year before against Detroit, they had all those penalties, and his whole idea coming in was to build a disciplined football team, so he didn't want to promote the perception that it wasn't disciplined by talking about penalties at that point. That's what he was mad about, and he sort of looked at me like I should know that because I coach a high school team, and I've been in the league, and all that stuff. I shouldn't ask him about that. I didn't think of it that way, so we went in and talked it over. We've had to do that a couple times.

I really had to become a wordsmith and phrase things the right way. It really isn't what you're asking, it's how you ask it that's the key, especially to somebody who's very emotional at that time. I told him, "Coach, there were a lot of times that I went in at halftime coaching my high school team that I wouldn't want anybody interviewing me during either." Things happen right at the end of the half, or you have a horrible first half, or they just haven't done everything they've done all week, or the officials have made calls you don't agree with. There are all those things that go into it, and that's a very emotional time. So I understood where he was coming from, but eventually he understood that I wasn't trying to put him on the stand and cross-examine him. That's not what I was trying to do.

CHAPTER 6
THE STEELERS

When the Ravens arrived in Baltimore in 1996, they found a natural rival in the Pittsburgh Steelers. They were two blue-collar cities with solid sports histories. Many people in Baltimore adopted the Steelers when the Colts left in 1984. There were many Western Pennsylvania natives who migrated to Maryland for jobs who remained Steelers fans. This meant thousands of black-and-gold Steelers fans waving their Terrible Towels each time their team played in Baltimore.

It was only fitting the Steelers handed the Ravens their first loss in the new franchise's history on September 8, 1996, with a dominant 31–17 victory at Three Rivers Stadium. Baltimore struggled mightily over its first year, but one of the highlights of the season was a 31–17 victory over the Steelers on December 1, 1996, at a rain-swept Memorial Stadium, snapping a four-game losing streak. Pittsburgh would still win the division at 10–6, while the Ravens finished last at 4–12. Nonetheless, a rivalry was being formed.

"This is a relief for the whole organization, and we beat 'em," Ravens coach Ted Marchibroda said after the game.

The loss against Baltimore apparently irked Pittsburgh, which then won the next five games in the series from 1997 to early 1999. The Steelers became another footnote in Baltimore football history when they handed the Ravens their first loss (20–13) at their new downtown stadium on September 6, 1998. Pittsburgh gave Baltimore a wake-up call and quashed the optimism of a 4–0 record in the preseason that had given fans a glimmer of hope of an improved team that might be capable of making the playoffs. The Steelers won the game despite being outgained 376 yards to 271. The game also spoiled the debut of

Baltimore defensive back Rod Woodson, who had played nine years in Pittsburgh.

"We certainly didn't play up to some standards offensively, but I thought we played pretty good defensively," Pittsburgh coach Bill Cowher said after the game. "The bottom line in this business is finding a way to win, and we were able to do that."

Unfortunately for the Ravens, they had consistently struggled to find that winning recipe at the time. That would slowly begin to change the following year. As the Ravens continued to improve, the games with Pittsburgh became more intense and were played for higher stakes. The Steelers had a classic rivalry with the Cleveland Browns, which was much closer geographically than Baltimore. The Ravens, though, were a team that was becoming a mirror image of Pittsburgh with their toughness, gritty play, and ability to pull out wins.

On December 12, 1999, the Ravens visited Pittsburgh as a steadily improving team under first-year coach Brian Billick, who had instilled a new confidence in his players. After some early struggles, the Ravens had won two of three games and were 5–7 as they entered a key game against the Steelers. A victory would bring Baltimore to within a game of being .500 this late in the season for the first time in the franchise's short history. The Ravens could also put themselves back in the playoff race with a win.

Baltimore responded with one of its best performances with a 31–24 victory. It was the first time the Ravens had won in Pittsburgh. Tony Banks showed glimpses that he could be a big-game quarterback by throwing for three touchdowns. Qadry Ismail had a Ravens–record 258 receiving yards, which was 11th best in the history of the NFL at the time.

The Ravens sealed the victory when running back Priest Holmes, who would later become a Pro-Bowl player with Kansas City, recovered the Steelers' onside kick. It was a monumental moment, as the tide appeared to be changing for the Ravens under Billick, who didn't hesitate when asked about what the game meant to the franchise and the big picture for the season.

"This organization, this group of guys, this team, this city, has never played a game in December in the last four years that could bring you to .500, that could have playoff ramifications," Billick said after the game. "Now, whether we get there or not, I don't know. But like I told the guys in there, you're not going to find out until you get to 9–7. Then we'll see. Someone will come and tell us if we're in the playoffs or not."

That game proved to be huge for the Ravens, who finished the season at 8–8—the first non-losing season since relocating to Baltimore. The Ravens carried that momentum into the 2000 season, and the first big test came in the season opener on September 3 with a road matchup against the Steelers, who were looking to avenge that previous loss.

Pittsburgh, however, encountered a completely different Ravens team. These Ravens had a different type of swagger and fearlessness. Despite facing an amped-up Steelers team and a raucous opening-day crowd at Three Rivers Stadium, Baltimore not only didn't flinch, it managed another dominant performance against their division rival.

The Ravens got the perfect start to their season with a 16–0 shutout that stunned both the Steelers and their fans. It was the first time the Ravens had ever held the Steelers scoreless, and it set the tone for the franchise's Super Bowl run. Banks threw a 53-yard touchdown pass to Qadry Ismail in the first quarter, and Matt Stover did the rest with three field goals. More than a victory, it was another boost to the Ravens' confidence. Pittsburgh would return the favor later in the season with a 9–6 victory at M&T Bank Stadium, but it would be the last loss for Baltimore that season.

The following year, the Ravens handed the Steelers their first loss at the newly opened Heinz Field on November 4. Pittsburgh kicker Kris Brown missed a 35-yard field goal attempt in the closing seconds, and the Ravens held on for the 13–10 victory. This game was the impetus of years of trash-talking between the two teams that ratcheted up the rivalry to a new dimension.

That loss stuck with the Steelers for weeks. Emotions were running high with the rematch in Baltimore on December 16. Pittsburgh receiver Plaxico Burress fired the first salvo when he said the Ravens were lucky to win the earlier game. "We beat those guys up physically," Burress said to the Pittsburgh beat reporters leading up to the game. "We know it. All we have to do is go down there and beat them up again this time and hopefully come out of there with a win."

Those comments did not sit well in Baltimore. The Ravens were the defending Super Bowl champions and still carried that swagger. Who better to fire back than outspoken tight end Shannon Sharpe, who was never afraid to back down from a war of words. Sharpe provided some great quotes to the Baltimore media: "I'm not even going to talk about Plaxico," Sharpe said. "I'm not even going to dignify what he said with a response. If [receiver] Hines Ward would have said that, as physical as he plays the game, okay, I could lend some credence to that. But Plexiglas? No."

The trash-talking didn't stop there. Steelers running back Jerome Bettis fanned the flames when he told a *Sports Illustrated* reporter that Cincinnati linebacker Takeo Spikes was as talented as Ray Lewis but Spikes did not have enough other playmakers around him like Lewis. Bettis was questionable for the game with a groin injury, but Lewis took exception to the comment and told Bettis to tape up, play the game, and "not run away from me." However, it was Sharpe who provided one of the best quotes of any player that season when he defended his teammate, who just happened to be the reigning Defensive Player of the Year.

"I think maybe [Bettis] had a concussion when he said that," Sharpe said. "Takeo is a great player, but Takeo is a Chevy and Ray is a Bentley. Now which one would you rather have? Comparing Takeo Spikes to Ray Lewis is like comparing a homeless man to Bill Gates. That's like saying *Dude, Where's My Car?* was just as good as *Titanic*. At some point in time, you've got to be realistic."

The Steelers, though, got their revenge with a 26–21 win in the Sunday night game and improved to 11–2 en route to the AFC North title. The Ravens finished in second place and took down Miami in the first round of the playoffs, setting up a rubber match against Pittsburgh in the AFC Divisional game. It was the first time the franchises had met in the postseason, which added more fuel to the rivalry. This time, Baltimore was no match for the Steelers, who rolled to a 27–10 victory. It was the most lopsided loss in the postseason of any defending champion in almost two decades. The Steelers didn't just beat the Ravens—they pushed them around. The game also ended the one-year tenure of Baltimore quarterback Elvis Grbac, who looked uneasy in the pocket most of the game and threw three interceptions.

It was a loss that would resonate with Baltimore throughout the offseason. Pittsburgh lost 24–17 to the eventual Super Bowl–champion New England Patriots in the AFC Championship game. The Ravens lamented not playing well enough to defend their title.

"They wanted it [more] than we did this year," Woodson said about Pittsburgh after the game. "That's disappointing. You need attitude on a football team to win. There's a fine line between cockiness and believing in yourself. I don't know what side of that fine line we were on this year."

The Steelers took advantage of the Ravens' rebuilding year in the newly aligned AFC North in 2002. Pittsburgh won both of the meetings that season, winning 31–18 at M&T Bank Stadium. Violence became another fixture in the rivalry when Ravens cornerback James Trapp stomped on Burress during a skirmish late in the second quarter. The Steelers won the division at 10–5–1, while Baltimore finished third at 7–9—the first losing season under Billick. Pittsburgh advanced to the AFC divisional round, losing to the Tennessee Titans 34–31 in overtime. The Ravens, meanwhile, picked themselves up and put an effective plan in place to rebound the following season.

The rivalry took on a new dimension when Baltimore drafted linebacker Terrell Suggs with the 10th overall pick in the 2003 NFL Draft. Suggs was a dominant pass rusher who was a perfect fit for Baltimore's aggressive defense. He wasted no time making an impact, setting the Ravens rookie record with 12 sacks. He was also named the NFL Defensive Rookie of the Year. Suggs was a quick learner and knew what the rivalry against Pittsburgh meant to the city of Baltimore. This endeared him to the Ravens' fans.

Suggs had an open disdain for Pittsburgh. He got a quick initiation into the rivalry during his first regular season game when the Ravens were dismantled 34–15. Baltimore recovered from the loss and entered the rematch with the Steelers in the regular season finale 9–6 and atop the division. Baltimore got its measure of revenge with a 13–10 overtime victory and the AFC North title.

The Ravens and Steelers split their regular season games the following two seasons before Baltimore earned the sweep in 2006. The teams split again the next season before the Steelers took full control of the rivalry again in three contentious meetings in 2008 when Suggs was at the center of a controversy. Weeks after a 23–20 overtime loss to Pittsburgh, Suggs told a radio show the Ravens had a bounty on wide receiver Hines Ward and running back Rashard Mendenhall. "The bounty was out on [Mendenhall] and the bounty was out on [Ward]," Suggs said on the "2 Live Stews" radio show. "We just didn't get him between the whistles."

This did not sit well with the NFL, which opened an investigation. Ward told *Pardon the Interference* on ESPN that having a bounty on his head was an honor, but it probably wasn't good for Suggs' future in the league. "All I have to say to Mr. Suggs is there's a policy in the NFL [against bounties] he should read," Ward said on the show. Suggs later backtracked on those statements, sensing a fine from the league.

"There wasn't any bounty," Suggs told the *Baltimore Sun*. "[The talk show host] asked me if there was a bounty, and I just said I'm going to keep a watch on the guy. [Ward] broke some guy's jaw last week, and he tried to cheap-shot [Jarret Johnson].

He has also cheap-shotted Ed Reed. We're just going to be on alert the next time we play him."

Suggs eventually got away with a warning. However, he had thrown down the gauntlet and carried the rivalry to a new level. The Steelers did most of their talking on the field, beating the Ravens again later that season 13–9 at M&T Bank Stadium. The Steelers won the AFC North with a 12–4 record, one game ahead of the 11–5 Ravens. This set up a showdown in the postseason. Pittsburgh gained the upper hand again and completed the three-game sweep with a 23–14 win in the AFC Championship game. Pittsburgh's defense led the way, as safety Troy Polamalu scored a 40-yard touchdown after intercepting Flacco. This also signaled another change in the rivalry. The teams' disdain for one another was turning into mutual respect.

"It was a typical, hard-hitting, physical game. It's the way every Baltimore–Pittsburgh game is," Ward said after the game. "Sometimes guys get hit so hard, you don't know if they're going to get up. They say defense wins championships. Well, we have the No. 1 defense. And they're the reason why we're really going to the Super Bowl."

The Ravens knew they had to start building a team that could take down their archrival on a consistent basis. Still, the teams split their regular season games again over the next two seasons. In 2010, they met for the second time in the playoffs. Once again, Pittsburgh made just enough plays to earn a 31–24 win in the AFC Divisional Round. The Ravens had three turnovers in the game but still had a chance to tie the game in the final minutes. However, Baltimore receiver T.J. Houshmandzadeh dropped an easy pass on a fourth-and-18 that could have extended a drive in Pittsburgh territory. "It's unbelievable," Houshmandzadeh said after the game. "I can't believe that happened. I would bet every dollar I have that I make that."

The reality was more heartbreak for the Ravens at the hands of their bitter rival. The two postseason losses were especially hard to swallow. However, few could deny the gap had been closed, and the Steelers and Ravens were almost mirror images of one another. Their matchups became must-watch TV for most of the country because of the hard hits and late-game drama. It was widely regarded as one of the best rivalries in the NFL. Baltimore, however, still had to figure out a way to gain a convincing edge. "We didn't put them away," Suggs said. "We have nobody to blame but ourselves. We have to take a long look at ourselves."

Baltimore bounced back from that loss with a series sweep in 2011. The teams split the following year, but the Ravens had more important things to focus on that season—primarily a run to their second Super Bowl victory. The Ravens were gaining the upper hand in the series, and finally it was Baltimore handing the Steelers some frustrating losses. From 2011 to 2016, the Ravens won nine of the 13 games against Pittsburgh. The tide had clearly turned, and mutual respect between the teams was at an all-time high for that rivalry.

Perhaps the Ravens' biggest victory over Pittsburgh arrived on January 3, 2015, in the AFC Wild Card game at Heinz Field. Most people were expecting more disappointment for Baltimore against Pittsburgh in the postseason. The Steelers had shown they knew how to win the biggest games against the Ravens. This time, Baltimore would finally emerge and earn one of the sweetest victories in franchise history.

The Ravens had endured a challenging season on and off the field. Running back Ray Rice was released from the team following a domestic abuse case with an incriminating video of the incident. Still, Harbaugh managed to steer the team through troubled waters to a 10–6 finish. The Ravens finished in third place in the AFC North, which sent three teams to playoffs that season, including the second-place Bengals.

The divisional rivalry continued in the postseason with the Steelers and Ravens meeting in the Wild Card round at Heinz Field. While Baltimore was the underdog, Harbaugh did his best to rally his players and handed out T-shirts prior to the game that read FAITH AND GUTS. It was a mantra embraced by the players.

The Ravens then did the rest of their talking on the field with a performance that stunned the Steelers and their yellow-towel-waving fans. Flacco tossed two second-half touchdowns as the Ravens pulled away from the Steelers 30–17 in the Wild Card game. That performance enhanced Flacco's legacy as a big-time player in the postseason and further endeared him to the fans by beating Pittsburgh. "This is a very special victory for us, not just because it's a playoff win," Harbaugh said after the game, "but because of who it comes against, which is our most respected rival."

The Ravens defense had allowed Steelers quarterback Ben Roethlisberger to throw six touchdown passes in the previous regular season meeting. This time, Roethlisberger was intercepted twice and sacked five times. It was also the first time an NFL team from Baltimore, including the old Colts, beat Pittsburgh in the postseason. The victory was another huge step for the Ravens as a franchise and another defining moment in this bitter rivalry.

"We played our best football game of the year right here, and I think it's because of what we've been through all year [and] the way we've stuck together," Harbaugh said. "We had each other's backs and maintained our faith. That's what has made the difference for us.... You don't let adversity get you down. Our guys have done that all year. You know over time that pays off."

Baltimore took control of the series by winning three consecutive games against Pittsburgh over the next two seasons. The Ravens finished just 5–11 in 2015, but two of those victories came against their biggest rival. The Steelers finally got their revenge on Christmas Day in 2016 with the division crown on the line.

Baltimore opened a 10-point lead in the second half before the Steelers fought back and pulled ahead. The Ravens answered and led 27–24 on a barreling 10-yard run by fullback Kyle Juszczyk with 1:18 left in the game. But that gave Roethlisberger just enough time to put together the game-winning 75-yard drive, capped when wide receiver Antonio Brown stretched the ball over the goal line with nine seconds remaining to seal the 31–27 win. The loss also knocked Baltimore out of the playoffs for the third time in four years.

Once again, Baltimore was forced to go into the offseason with a bitter taste in its mouth because of Pittsburgh. Still, the Ravens knew the rivalry would commence again the following season. The players might change here and there, but the intensity will stay the same.

"It's disappointing," Flacco said. "I don't know what else to say besides that. Disappointed is disappointed. We had it right there. Obviously, we still have to go play next week. We had to win here tonight and then win there, too. It wasn't all right there but we played good football today. It is football. It's just football at the end of the day. You play 60 minutes for a reason, and sometimes you just can't get it done."

As long as Baltimore and Pittsburgh maintain some level of success on the field, the rivalry between the two franchises will remain one of the best in the NFL. What began as a lopsided affair evolved into an acrimonious relationship between the teams. Over the past few years, that hatred has turned into a mutual respect, and there is less banter between the players leading up to the game. Instead, the teams are prepared for the most intense, hard-hitting game of the season that will likely go down to the final play of the game.

"It's hard to describe," Harbaugh said about the rivalry with Pittsburgh. "It's like a lot of things; you know it when you see it and when you're a part of it and when you live it. It's something I've really grown to love. It's rough, tough, disciplined, hard-nosed. It's really everything football is supposed to be. To me, that's what makes it special."

STAN'S SIDEBAR

ON THE BALTIMORE-PITTSBURGH RIVALRY

I was part of the Ohio State–Michigan rivalry as a player and as a father. Ohio State–Michigan and Baltimore-Pittsburgh are two of the great rivalries. Now, Ohio State–Michigan goes back so much further. It's got more history, and there are a lot of alumni from both of those universities who hate each other. This is the local Ohio State–Michigan rivalry, that's for sure. That's what it is. They don't like each other. They respect each other. Let's just say the Steelers, if they had to pick a team, wouldn't pick the Ravens to play, if it was a big game. And I think the Ravens would pick the Steelers to play.

Two years ago, Cincinnati played Pittsburgh, and the Ravens had to play the winner of that game. I was rooting for Pittsburgh to beat Cincinnati because we've always had problems with Cincinnati, for some reason, especially in Cincinnati, but we had been able to go into Pittsburgh and beat them. We should have beaten them in late 2016. But the Ravens have always been able to get themselves ready mentally to compete with Pittsburgh at every level, and I think Pittsburgh knows that. I think they match up with them mentally and physically, especially mentally. I don't think Cincinnati wants to play Pittsburgh and, for me, I don't want to play Cincinnati. For some reason, the Ravens have had more problems with Cincinnati. I was doing an appearance with Joe Flacco this year for the Y's of Maryland, and one of the questions they asked from the audience was, 'Who do you really want to beat?" And he said, "I know everybody expects me to say Pittsburgh, but I really want to beat Cincinnati, because we've had a hard time beating them."

For some reason, what Cincinnati coach Marvin Lewis does gives Joe a problem. Joe is locked in on what Pittsburgh does. He finds the weaknesses of their defense. Marvin seems to come up with a different game plan or something different every time that somehow throws Joe off whack. He really plays well against Pittsburgh, and he does not play as well against Cincinnati, and I think he realizes that, and that's why if he had to pick a team he wanted to beat, it's Cincinnati.

CHAPTER 7
JOE COOL

Quarterback Joe Flacco was the Ravens' first-round pick (18th overall) in the 2008 NFL Draft. The Ravens finally found their franchise quarterback after spending the early years trying to find an effective, consistent starter. The strong-armed Flacco is one of the only starting quarterbacks in NFL history (since the 1970 merger) to win a playoff game in each of his first five seasons (2008–12). He is also the Ravens' all-time passing leader.

One of the biggest challenges for the Ravens in their early history was finding a franchise quarterback who could consistently help the team fight for divisional titles and become a perennial Super Bowl contender. When the Ravens arrived in Baltimore in 1996, the team had strong-armed Vinny Testaverde behind center. Testaverde, however, was entering his 10th season in the league, so he was already on the back side of his career. Still, Testaverde managed to have two solid seasons in Baltimore, throwing for 4,177 yards with 33 touchdowns. He was voted to the Pro Bowl in the team's inaugural season—still the only Ravens quarterback to earn that honor. The following year, however, he missed three games and was later released by the team.

From there, Baltimore had a revolving door at quarterback, which coincided with the team's struggles on the field. The Ravens managed to find a successful formula that entailed putting together a stellar defense complemented by a serviceable quarterback who could avoid costly, game-changing mistakes. No other quarterback embodied that role better than Trent Dilfer, who made just enough plays to help the Ravens win the Super Bowl in 2000.

Still, the Ravens brass knew it would be difficult to maintain success and make ensuing runs to the Super Bowl without an upper-echelon quarterback to lead the offense. The pressure to find this player also led to poor front office decisions, most notably the signing of Elvis Grbac prior to the 2001 season to replace Super Bowl–winning quarterback Trent Dilfer.

From 1996 until Joe Flacco was drafted in 2008, the Ravens had 15 different starting quarterbacks: Testaverde (1996–97), Eric Zeier (1997–98), Jim Harbaugh (1998), Tony Banks (1999–2000),

Stoney Case (1999), Scott Mitchell (1999), Dilfer (2000), Grbac (2001), Randall Cunningham (2001), Jeff Blake (2002), Chris Redman (2002), Anthony Wright (2003, 2005), Kyle Boller (2003–05, 2007), Steve McNair (2006–07), and Troy Smith (2007).

That changed with the selection of Flacco with the 18th overall pick in the 2008 NFL Draft. The quarterback position became even more critical when McNair announced his retirement in April 2008. Baltimore considered drafting Matt Ryan out of Boston College, but he was taken by the Atlanta Falcons with the third overall pick. Baltimore would have had to give too much to move up that far in the draft. The Ravens were impressed with Flacco after they watched him work out at the University of Delaware, when he had no trouble throwing the ball downfield on a windy day. Baltimore maneuvered around before landing him, first moving from the 8th overall pick to 26th and then back up to 18th. "We decided it was time to pull the trigger on the quarterback that we felt was the guy to lead our football team into the future," Newsome said.

Flacco was a strong-armed quarterback from then-Division I-AA Delaware. He had originally started at the University of Pittsburgh but transferred to get more playing time and improve his stock for the NFL. In two seasons at Delaware, Flacco threw for 7,046 yards with 41 touchdowns and 15 interceptions. Despite playing just two years, Flacco set 20 Blue Hens passing records, including completions (595), attempts (938), 200-yard passing games (21), consecutive 200-yard passing games (15), 300-yard passing games (11), and consecutive pass attempts without an interception (212).

"I think I'm a strong kid who can hang in the pocket and throw the ball accurately with people around him," Flacco said in a conference call with reporters after he was drafted. "I think a big part of being a good quarterback is being an accurate passer and being an accurate passer under pressure. So a lot of people say arm strength [is important] and everything like that, but I don't think it's the most important thing about playing quarterback. I definitely think it helps me in making some of the throws. But like I said, I think the important thing is being good in the pocket and being accurate within that pocket."

At 6'6" and 245 pounds, Flacco had the perfect frame for a quarterback. While the team was confident Flacco could challenge Troy Smith and Boller for a starting role his rookie year, the Ravens were just as happy to let him spend the year learning the system. However, Smith, a former Heisman Trophy Award winner, missed most of the preseason with tonsillitis, and Boller was dealing with a shoulder injury. This catapulted Flacco into the starting role.

Flacco had some challenges in the early part of the season, throwing for just two touchdowns with seven interceptions over seven games. Players and fans questioned whether Flacco was ready to lead the offense. Linebacker Terrell Suggs even went on an Atlanta radio station questioning Coach Harbaugh's decision to keep Flacco behind center, especially with Smith able to play. "Right now, I think [Flacco is] all right," Suggs said. "But like I said, in the end, Troy should be the starter [because he's] the better man for the job." That type of criticism would be tough for any quarterback, especially a rookie. But Flacco had a steely demeanor and was not affected by outside distractions.

Harbaugh maintained his confidence in the young quarterback and kept him behind center throughout the season.

"He has come so far, but he was pretty good coming in," Harbaugh said. "And he was our quarterback day one, and he remains our quarterback now—whatever day this is. He's a guy we believe in. We don't put tags on guys. We don't see guys as being rookies or whatever. They're ours. They're Ravens. And we're proud of guys who play like Ravens, and we think Joe plays like a Raven."

The move paid off, as Flacco threw for 12 touchdowns and five interceptions over the final eight games. Baltimore went 7–2 over that stretch and finished in second place in the AFC North, advancing to the AFC Championship game where the Reavens lost to Pittsburgh. Overall, Flacco had a phenomenal rookie season and was named the 2008 Diet Pepsi Rookie of the Year. He also became the first rookie quarterback in NFL history to win two playoff games.

Flacco had earned the name "Joe Cool" because of his demeanor and ability to remain calm under pressure. This also earned him the respect of his teammates—even Suggs, who had criticized Flacco earlier in the year. Flacco was an ultimate team player and took responsibility for his mistakes and credited teammates when the Ravens had success. Most importantly, Baltimore had found a long-term solution at quarterback. Flacco was ready to embrace that role even on a veteran-laden team.

"It makes it easy for me to feel like I actually do fit in and gives me the confidence to go out there and play the way I need to," Flacco said in a conference call with reporters late in the season. "Those guys have been like that from day one. They've never made me feel out of place. As soon as I came in here, they've done all they can to make sure I feel comfortable on this team, and all I need to think about is going out there and playing the way I need to. That's the biggest thing with those guys. They've been kind enough to do that, and it gives me the confidence to just go out there and play and not have to worry about all the other little things."

Flacco had continued success the following years, leading the Ravens to the playoffs over the next five seasons. In 15 postseason games, Flacco went 10–5 with 3,223 yards, along with 25 touchdowns and 10 interceptions. The 10 wins, including seven on the road, were the most of any active quarterback at the time. He also had a quarterback rating of 88.6 over that stretch. Flacco has also produced perhaps the biggest play in franchise history with the "Mile High Miracle"—the 70-yard touchdown pass to Jacoby Jones against the Broncos.

"It's no different," Flacco said about the playoffs compared to the regular season. "It's going out there and playing a football game. I'm doing the best I can to put everybody in a position to do good things, put the ball in their hands and let them take over. I think we've just come together and played well as a unit."

He continued: "In the regular season, the cliché line is one play at a time, one game at a time At this point [with the playoffs], you really are. You don't have any choice but to be totally locked in on this one game. There's nothing really to look forward to. You don't know what's going to happen after this. It's definitely an interesting mind-set that you take as a team, and it's a lot of fun."

Several months after he led the team to the Super Bowl victory in 2012, the Ravens showed their confidence in Flacco by signing him a six-year, $120.6 million contract, which made him the highest-paid player in the league. Baltimore had an opportunity to extend Flacco earlier but decided to let him play out his original contract. Flacco was set to become an unrestricted free agent and the front office had to work out deal, which cost them millions of extra dollars. That huge contract also brought more responsibility and increased scrutiny on the quarterback. Flacco was expected to carry the team with that type of salary, which also precluded the Ravens from investing heavily in other positions.

However, Flacco faced the biggest adversity of his career in 2015. Entering that season, he had started every regular season game since he was drafted by the team. But on November 22, 2015, Flacco suffered a major injury for the first time in his career when he tore both his ACL and MCL against the St. Louis Rams. Flacco was injured with 54 seconds remaining in the game when Rams defensive end Matt Longacre pushed left tackle James Hurst into Flacco's left leg. Flacco showed his toughness by staying in the game for three more plays, setting up a 47-yard field goal by Justin Tucker for a 16–13 win. Still, his season was over and the Ravens never recovered.

After the game, Harbaugh announced that Flacco was officially out for the year, opening the door for backup Ryan Mallett to start. The players and coaches were devastated. Up to that point, Flacco had appeared in 137 consecutive games, which was the second-longest streak in NFL history by a quarterback to begin a career behind Peyton Manning.

"I'm probably still in shock a little bit," Flacco said after the game. "You play football and you play as long as I have and you play as hard as we do out there, then stuff like this happens. You have to just stand tall and be tough about it. That's all you can do. I think that's the way I am about everything in my life, and I'm not going to be any different this time."

The Ravens were already struggling that season, and without Flacco there was little hope to salvage the year. Baltimore finished 5–11—its worst mark under Harbaugh—and missed the playoffs for the second time in three years. The biggest question was whether Flacco would be ready for the 2016 season. The pressure was on the organization to bounce back from recent struggles and get back in the playoff hunt.

The team faced an uphill battle for a quick turnaround. Baltimore endured several key injuries in 2015. In addition to Flacco, wide receiver Steve Smith, linebacker Terrell Suggs, and running back Justin Forsett each suffered season-ending injuries. All of those players were veterans, and there was uncertainty about how well they would recover. The Ravens were also hampered by their salary cap, especially with so much money tied up in Flacco. These issues had to be addressed in the offseason.

In March 2016, Flacco helped the process by signing a three-year contract extension worth $66.4 million, including a $40 million signing bonus and $44 million in guaranteed money. He once again became the highest-paid player in the league. However, the contract was structured in a way that provided some salary cap relief, allowing Baltimore to fix other areas of the team. The Ravens desperately needed help in their injury-plagued secondary and needed another dynamic wide receiver that could pose a threat downfield.

Despite the hefty investment, the Ravens were happy to lock up Flacco for the long term. The team needed to move forward with a franchise quarterback, and Newsome was confident that Flacco was the answer. There were no second thoughts about offering the extension—at least publicly.

"On his shoulders stands the success of this organization over the last eight years," Newsome said. "There aren't many opportunities that you can draft a quarterback and for him to have the success that he, along with John [Harbaugh], have had over the first eight years of their career. In spending time with numerous GMs over the last week over at the combine, they all dread the day when they don't have a quarterback, and what you have to do to go and get one. We're fortunate to have one. In my mind, having Joe for the next six years, I think his best football is still ahead of him."

Flacco worked hard in the offseason to ensure he was ready for 2016. He impressed player personnel and his coaches with his work ethic. By the time training camp rolled around in August, Flacco was ready to take the ball and resume his starting responsibilities. The Ravens signed receiver Mike Wallace in the offseason to provide Flacco with another downfield threat. Another wide receiver—Breshad Perriman, the team's first-round pick in 2015—was also back on the field after missing his entire rookie season with a knee injury.

The result, however, was another subpar season where the Ravens finished just 8–8. Flacco did not have any setbacks physically, but he appeared hesitant in the pocket when he felt pressure. Still, Flacco set the franchise record with 4,317 passing yards. He also threw 20 touchdowns with 15 interceptions. In the end, Baltimore missed the playoffs for the third time in four seasons, and Flacco was at the center of the criticism because he was expected to be the leader of the team.

Despite the struggles, the Ravens were within one play of being in position to win the division. Those hopes were dashed Christmas Day against the Steelers in a 31–27 loss. Steelers wide receiver Antonio Brown scored the winning touchdown when he stretched the ball over the goal line with nine seconds left. But Flacco remained confident Baltimore could still rebound and become playoff contenders once again.

"You just live year by year, and you live in your own little world," Flacco told reporters after the game. "Every year is a grind—mentally, physically, everything about it. We leave it all out there on the field. It obviously feels good to go into the playoffs and to win a game in the playoffs. But honestly, we have had one year that felt good at the end of it. That was when we won the Super Bowl. Other than that, we all feel about the same way we feel right now.

"It does not matter that you got to an AFC Championship in that given year. We still lost. At the end of the day, it is really no better than being 8–8. It is all or nothing in this league. At some point, you feel pretty crappy about how your year went, and there is one team at the end of it every year that doesn't."

STAN'S SIDEBAR

ON JOE FLACCO

We were talking about Joe on the pre-game show recently. Ray Lewis said something about Flacco, and I was defending him, saying, "That's his personality, that's the way it is." A former Colts secretary sent me a text and she said, "You know what? They used to say the same thing about Johnny Unitas, that he didn't show any emotions, that he was just stoic all the time.

Now here we're doing it again against the two best quarterbacks Baltimore's ever had—Johnny Unitas and Joe Flacco." You can put Bert Jones in that category, too.

Joe has won. That's what a quarterback's job is—to win. It's not to have the best completion percentage or the highest quarterback rating or any of that. Philip Rivers has that every year, and the Chargers never go to the playoffs. Philip Rivers, Matt Ryan, Tony Romo, all these guys have these great quarterback ratings but they don't win, and the quarterback's job is to win. And sometimes you have to sacrifice those things to win. You get a little bit more conservative. You throw here because you know your defense is so good you don't need to take any chances, and you shouldn't take any chances, even if it hurts your individual statistics, because that's what's best for the team to win. And that's the way Joe has been his whole time here.

He's a winner. And yes, he's a leader. When you perform, you become a leader. At the quarterback position, you're going to be a leader one way or the other. Either you're going to lead them downhill or you're going to lead them uphill. Because Joe performs, he wins. When you need a big play, he'll hit Jacoby Jones down the middle. He'll hit Dennis Pitta from his own 3-yard line in overtime in the playoffs against Denver. He'll make the play that you have to make to win a football game. First of all, he's got the arm. He's got an unbelievable arm. He can throw it as long as he wants. He can throw it as hard as he wants.

They talk about him throwing off his back foot, but he's one of the few guys who has the arm to be able to do that. I forget what the percentage is, but it's over 50 percent of the time that quarterbacks have to throw under pressure in this league. So you better be able to do that well, throw off your back foot or throw without being able to step into it, those types of things, because the pressure's right in your face. He has that, and he's smart, and he's willing to sacrifice his own statistics for the good of the team.

That's what's most important for a quarterback. I played against and with a lot of quarterbacks who would throw the easy pass on third down just to get statistics, even though it may be a five-yard pass when you need eight yards. They'll take the ones given to them rather than try to stick it in downfield where you need to make the play. There are a lot of quarterbacks who are not willing to sacrifice their own statistics for the good of the team. Joe is.

CHAPTER 8
CRISIS MANAGEMENT

The Baltimore Ravens have dealt with several controversies during their history, most notably the Ray Lewis murder trial, the Jamal Lewis drug case, and the Ray Rice domestic abuse situation. The Ravens, however, directly addressed each of these issues head-on and none of them overshadowed the team. Through these trials and tribulations, Baltimore showed it is a model organization for crisis management.

Ray Lewis was the first major scandal when he was indicted for murder after a fight broke out on January 31, 2000, following a Super Bowl party in Atlanta at 4:00 AM. Jacinth Baker and Richard Lollar were stabbed to death in the melee. In addition to Lewis, Reginald Oakley and Joseph Sweeting were also indicted on murder and aggravated assault charges. However, the evidence was spotty, and a knife found near the scene of the crime did not have any fingerprints on it. An alleged bloody white suit worn by Lewis was never found.

Lewis was indicted on murder and aggravated assault charges and spent several weeks in jail. He pleaded guilty to misdemeanor charge of obstruction of justice in exchange for his testimony against Oakley and Sweeting. Lewis received 12 months of probation and was fined $250,000 by the NFL. "He was an innocent man, wrongly accused, who's been through an awful ordeal," Ray Lewis' attorney, Ed Garland, told reporters after his client was acquitted on the murder charges. "Today he has been exonerated." Both Oakley and Sweeting were later acquitted of murder charges. No one else has been arrested for the murder of Baker and Lollar, and the case remains unsolved.

The Ravens organization, most notably owner Art Modell and coach Brian Billick, stood by Lewis throughout the murder trial.

"The players are obviously excited to have this behind them, keeping all this in the context that two people are dead," Billick said after Lewis was given probation. "What we're here to do now is move beyond this." When Lewis eventually returned to Baltimore, the team hosted a press conference attended by the national and local media where Lewis read a statement and even answered questions. The move was expected to address the issue directly and clear the cloud hovering over the team. However, it became increasingly difficult to move beyond the controversy with each victory the following season.

When the Ravens reached Super Bowl XXXV in Tampa, Florida, a scrum of reporters were there to meet Lewis and rehash the murder trial and the unsolved case. Billick, a former public relations intern with the San Francisco 49ers, was fully ready to take on the media and defend his player. Billick wasted no time addressing about 200 reporters seeking answers. "As much as some of you want to, we are not going to retry this," Billick said at the time, remarks that made national headlines. "It's inappropriate, and you're not qualified." Billick made it clear the team was not going to spend its week preparing for the biggest game in franchise history by rehashing a year-old murder trial where Lewis was cleared of the murder charges.

Billick continued: "To begin with, it's important to note that all the charges were dropped against Ray Lewis. There was no plea bargaining. It became very apparent to the D.A. because it was very apparent to anybody that witnessed the proceeding that Ray's involvement in that [incident] did not warrant the accusations or the charges. That's why they were dropped. Ray, after the charges were dropped, offered to testify. He admitted readily to having not handled the situation the way he wished he had, in terms of not dealing with police in a forthright manner. And it was dealt with at a misdemeanor level. These are the facts. You can stir it up, you can talk about it, but you're not going to change the facts."

While Billick was widely criticized, the Ravens players followed their coach's lead and were defiant in the face of the media and laser-focused on the game. Baltimore dismantled New York 34–7 and Lewis was named the game's Most Valuable Player. Baltimore had prevailed through the crisis, and many teams would use that approach as a model to deal with their own controversies.

Ray Lewis could do it all at linebacker—often with a bit of flash and dash attached. He had the speed to cover receivers and the power to knock a runner three yards backward. Lewis led the Baltimore defense for many years, helping the Ravens win two Super Bowl titles, and he will be in the Hall of Fame soon.

Lewis has always proclaimed his innocence. In his autobiography, *I Feel Like Going On: Life, Game and Glory*, Lewis wrote: "The charges made no sense. Told myself, that district attorney, he would suffer for this. Told myself, *Ray, you got praying folks in your corner.* That was my mind-set at the time. I came at this thing from a place of rage, a place of revenge. But in the end, *I* would be the one to suffer. Those poor boys, they paid the ultimate price, how many things went down for them that night. But me, I was made to pay for their deaths. In the court of public opinion, I was made to pay. In the detention facilities of the city of Atlanta, Georgia, I was made to pay. I was crucified, man." Lewis overcame the controversy. A statue of his likeness stands outside the Ravens' stadium, next to Johnny Unitas. Unfortunately, the families of Jacinth Baker and Richard Lollar are still searching for answers.

Baltimore was blindsided by another legal issue in February 2004 when running back Jamal Lewis was charged with conspiracy and possession with the intent to distribute at least five kilograms of cocaine. Lewis had been the team's first-round pick, fifth overall, in the 2000 NFL Draft and was emerging as one of the top runners in the NFL. Now he was looking at time in prison if found guilty of the charges. Garland, who also defended Ray Lewis, proclaimed the running back's innocence. "Mr. Lewis wants everybody to know that he did nothing wrong," Garland told the media at the time. "He was not part of any drug deal and any connection that he was was false.'"

The Ravens also defended their player, issuing a statement: "We believe in due process, and Jamal will have his day in court. There are two sides to every story. From what we know of the charges, these seem out of character for the Jamal we know." This type of loyalty gained the respect of Lewis' teammates, and the Ravens continued to boost their reputation as a signature franchise that looked after its own. Jamal Lewis eventually reached a plea agreement and agreed to serve four months in jail plus two months in a halfway house. He was also fined $200,000 and ordered to perform 500 hours of community service.

"We believe we did the right thing. There are no regrets," Garland told the media after the agreement. "Faced with the situation again, we wouldn't do anything differently. Jamal Lewis has got his life and his career back. I think he's ready to get it over with."

The Ravens were happy to get past another controversy and get back to concentrating on football. It would be 10 years before more storm clouds emerged again. This time, the situation would significantly alter how the franchise dealt with player personnel issues as well as the way the NFL handles domestic abuse situations.

On February 15, 2014, Ray Rice was arrested following a physical altercation with his fiancée, Janay Palmer, at the Revel Casino in Atlantic City. At the time, Rice's attorney called the incident a "minor physical altercation" and there was little scrutiny over the incident. However, surveillance video at the hotel captured the incident, showing Rice dragging Palmer out of the elevator by her hair. The footage was released by the gossip website TMZ.

The Ravens initially stood by Rice after the arrest, walking a thin line between loyalty to their player and understanding the severity of the incident. Harbaugh said: "The two people obviously have a couple issues that they have to work through, and they're both committed to doing that. That was the main takeaway for me from the conversation. They understand their own issues. They're getting a lot of counseling and those kinds of things, so I think that's really positive. That was the main takeaway."

On March 27, 2014, Rice was indicted by a grand jury for third-degree aggravated assault. Two months later, Rice was accepted into a pretrial intervention program focused on rehabilitation, and he avoided a trial. The aggravated assault charge would be dropped upon successful completion of the year-long program. Rice was also suspended for two games by the NFL—a move widely criticized for not being severe enough on domestic abuse. NFL Commissioner Roger Goodell would later mandate a six-game suspension for NFL personnel who violate the league's policy on assault, battery, domestic violence, and sexual assault. Players who violate the policy twice now face a lifetime ban. But the controversy over Rice and the incident was still far from over.

On September 8, 2014, TMZ released a second video. This time, the footage showed Rice knocking out Palmer inside the elevator with a blow to the head before dragging her out of the elevator by her hair. There was an overwhelming sense of outrage about the severity of the situation. The Ravens cut Rice later that day, but the team was still at the center of the criticism.

A report by ESPN alleged the Ravens knew about the longer video before it surfaced publicly. The story also alleged Coach Harbaugh wanted to cut Rice shortly after the incident, but the front office ruled against him. Both Bisciotti and Harbaugh denied those allegations, and the Ravens issued an eight-page rebuttal to the ESPN report.

After a road victory against the Cleveland Browns, the Ravens were met by a throng of local and national media waiting for answers. Baltimore later held a formal press conference attended by Bisciotti to deal with the controversy head-on. While both the Ravens and the NFL said they had never seen the video from inside the elevator prior to it being made public, Bisciotti admitted the team would have handled the situation differently if given another chance.

"I'm sorry that we didn't push harder to get that tape," Bisciotti said. "It seems to me in hindsight that we certainly had the leverage to say to Ray and his lawyer that we can't have him play on our team until we see that last bit of evidence. That's what we are dealing with now."

Meanwhile, Harbaugh was trying to run the daily operations of his football team. The controversy with Rice certainly was a distraction for the coaches and the players. Harbaugh lauded his personnel for staying focused amid the growing storm. Baltimore would finish the season 10–6 and earn a spot in the postseason

"When you're in football, you get pretty used to being under attack," Harbaugh said at the press conference with the owner. "You can't worry about it. You have to try to do what's right and do your best."

The Rice controversy had a lasting effect on the way the Ravens handle players. The team now makes it a priority to attract high-caliber players who avoid off-the-field issues. This created a problem as the team looked to get back in the upper echelon of the league after an 8–8 season in 2016. Should the team not pursue a top playmaker if he has questionable character? There was a fine line to find that answer. The .500 finish meant Baltimore had missed the playoffs three times in the past four years. Still, the Ravens remained confident they could win by balancing on-the-field performance with solid off-the-field behavior

"We weigh the risks," Newsome said at the team's annual season-ending news conference on January 10, 2016. "Within this organization, we have a lot of people that have been around athletes that have had issues, but when we take a player, especially through the draft, then we come up with a plan of what that player needs—not only on the football field, but off the field. I don't think we're afraid of 'character guys,' but we want guys that, No. 1, love to play football, that are going to be here on time, and hopefully not get in trouble when they leave.

"But we have to do any and everything that we can with 21- and 22- and 23-year-old athletes to help them so that they can go from being a young Ray Lewis or a young Jamal Lewis, who had issues, to end up being stellar leaders within the organization. We're not afraid of that. I think there are good players that don't have character issues. Ronnie Stanley is a real good football player, and he doesn't have any character issues. But we're not afraid of it. When we do take someone, it's on all of us to make sure that guy is doing everything he needs to do to change his life."

STAN'S SIDEBAR

ON RAY LEWIS

Ray is a complex person, to say the least. In my estimation, he is one of the two greatest inside linebackers to ever play the game. Dick Butkus, No. 1, Ray Lewis, No. 2, and as I told Ray, I've got to give him an edge because he played 17 years and Butkus played eight or nine years. But Butkus was so far ahead of his time because he was a 250-pound linebacker when the linemen weren't that big.

You know, Ray was a 240-pound linebacker when he was playing against 300-pounders. He was good because he was smart. Obviously, he had the physical capacity. He could run, he could hit, he could take on blockers. He knew all those things to do. But a lot of people have the physical capability. It's having that mental aspect of being able to take your film study onto the field and be able to know what the other team is going to do before they do it. And that gives you that great first step. You are in control then.

If you get the right step as a linebacker, you are way ahead. If you get the wrong first step, you better be very, very good to come back from that. He knew where the play was going. He knew when a screen was coming, He knew if they were going to pass or run in certain situations. He could read offensive linemen. He could read backs and the way they set up—all those things. I know this because that's the only way I could survive; I wasn't nearly as fast or as strong as Ray Lewis and maybe didn't need to be in that era, but I still had to be a step ahead because I wasn't going to catch O.J. Simpson from behind or Walter Payton or any of those guys I had to cover or play against. So my whole theory was to know where they're going, go over there, and wait for them. Don't try to run with them while they're going there; be a step ahead of them.

Ray was always a step ahead of them, and he had great physical skills and was able to come up with big plays at big times. And he was willing to gamble when he knew what was coming. Like that fourth-down play against San Diego when he ran through the line when he shouldn't have. But he made the play. He had seen the film study that the double-team was supposed to come off on him but it was coming off on the outside, so he went to the inside of it, where the center blocked back. He went right between the center and the guard. But he had to do it real quick, because all they had to do was get one little bump on him and he's out, and that means they're a player short. He knew where to go, and he made the great play.

You're always just part of the reason. He was the guy who made the other 10 players better. Eric Weddle does that now. But you better be really good yourself, too, for them to listen to you. You can't be a leader unless you perform. Performance matters in the NFL.

You can't be the rah-rah guy—if you aren't performing, they don't listen. It's like I say with a coach. If you don't win, they aren't going to listen to you. If you're a player, if you don't play, nobody listens to you. If you make plays and you help other guys make plays, you get a lot of respect in the league, and Ray always did that. He made the other 10 guys on the field better.

You could see when he came back for the playoffs in 2012, and Haloti Ngata came back, and Ed Reed came back. They just made an unbelievable run, and retiring was part of that, too. They all wanted to win for him, too, on top of that. That doesn't play much into it when you're playing. But it does when you're preparing.

Guys prepare harder when there's more on the line. Like I said, preparation is the key. So they'll study extra film, they'll remember it better, all of those things. I always liked to see Ray before the play, pointing out things. He was telling people where to go. He's moving linemen. Then to watch him slowly move right before the snap and at the snap and take that first step—it was always interesting to watch him because 80, 90 percent of the time, he was right.

CHAPTER 9
ART MODELL

Art Modell was a successful, self-made businessman from Brooklyn, New York. Ambitious, street-savvy, and entrepreneurial before that word was even part of American vernacular, Modell made his mark in advertising and public relations. In 1961, Modell invested some of the funds he had made over the years to buy a professional football team, the Cleveland Browns, for $4 million. This began a long relationship with the citizens of northeast Ohio.

The relationship burgeoned early, with the Browns winning the 1964 NFL championship over the Baltimore Colts. Few would have predicted at the time that would be the last NFL title for Cleveland under Modell. The league, however, was steadily growing, and Modell was widely considered a pioneer who helped expand the game.

Modell served as the league president from 1967 to 1969, helping negotiate the first collective bargaining agreement with the players. He helped broker the deal for the NFL-AFL Merger Committee. A deadlock in the negotiations was broken when Modell agreed to move the Browns to the AFC, creating an overall stronger league. Modell was also the NFL's broadcast chairman, laying the foundation for the lucrative television contracts the league enjoys today. His negotiations with TV networks for the league spanned three decades. Modell played a vital role in the launch of *Monday Night Football*, and as a reward, the Browns hosted the New York Jets in the first-ever game, earning a 31–21 victory.

On the field, the Browns were a model NFL franchise, routinely packing Cleveland Municipal Stadium, which Modell took full ownership of in 1973. The Browns advanced to the playoffs just twice in the 1970s, losing to the Colts in 1971 and the Dolphins the following year. Cleveland then endured an eight-year postseason drought until 1980 when it lost to the Oakland Raiders in the divisional round.

The rest of the 1980s were full of hope and some of the worst heartbreak of any NFL franchise. The Browns advanced to the postseason seven of 10 years but could never get over the hump to earn a trip to the Super Bowl. Two of the playoff losses are forever etched in the minds of Cleveland football fans and are so painful, both are each remembered by two words: "The Drive" and "The Fumble."

On January 11, 1987, the Browns hosted the Denver Broncos in the AFC championship game. Cleveland had controlled most of the game and held a 20–13 lead with five minutes left in the game. The Browns had a chance to close out the game when they backed up the Broncos to their own 2-yard line on what could have been their final possession of the game. Instead, Denver quarterback John Elway methodically picked apart the Cleveland defense, going the 98 yards for the game-tying touchdown. This became known as "The Drive," capped by a five-yard pass to Mark Jackson. Elway continued his masterful performance in overtime and drove the Broncos back down the field to set up a winning 33-yard field goal by Rich Karlis. It was a devastating loss that haunts Browns fans to this day.

The following year brought even more heartbreak. Cleveland appeared to have bounced back from the disappointment of the playoff loss to the Broncos, winning the AFC Central with a 10–5 record. The Browns rolled over the Indianapolis Colts 38–21 in the divisional round of the playoffs to set up another showdown with Denver in the AFC championship. A victory would cure all of Cleveland's wounds from "The Drive." Instead, the Broncos gutted the franchise once again.

Playing in front of a raucous crowd at Mile High Stadium, Denver jumped out to a 21–3 lead at the half. However, Browns quarterback Bernie Kosar led a furious second-half rally and eventually helped tie the game at 31–31. Elway, who had become Cleveland's No. 1 nemesis, put together a 75-yard scoring drive that gave the Broncos the lead once again.

With 3:53 left in the game, it was up to Kosar to match Elway's heroics. The Cleveland quarterback got his team down to the 8-yard line...and then the inexplicable happened. The Browns' sure-handed running back Ernest Byner took a handoff and appeared to have a seam to the end zone. Instead, he was stripped of the ball by Broncos defensive back Jeremiah Castille, who then pounced on "The Fumble" at the 3-yard line. Denver then held on for the 38–33 victory. It was another devastating loss that would haunt Modell and the Browns franchise for years to come. Byner was affected most by the gaffe and was prominently featured in an ESPN documentary titled "Believeland," which chronicles the ups and downs of Cleveland's sports history.

"I messed it up. I messed it up for everyone," Byner says through tears in the documentary. "I love the game. I loved playing for you all. And I'm sorry for letting you down."

The 1990s brought a new era of Browns football and a much more challenging economic climate in Cleveland. The Cleveland Indians, who paid Modell rent to play at Cleveland Municipal Stadium, had become disillusioned with the lease agreement and revenue sharing. This prompted the franchise to pursue public funds for a new stadium. Voters in Cuyahoga County eventually rejected a proposal for a publicly funded domed stadium, which would have been home to both the Browns and Indians. Instead, the project evolved and voters eventually agreed to a tax on alcohol and cigarettes to help finance the Gateway Sports and Entertainment Complex. This development included a new stadium for the Indians and an arena for the Cleveland Cavaliers in the NBA. There are still conflicting reports over whether the Browns were invited to be part of the project.

Either way, this created a significant new hurdle for the Browns. The franchise lost a key tenant for a stadium that was already struggling to remain financially viable because it was falling apart. There were also no corporate luxury boxes, which had become a key source of revenue for other NFL franchises. On the field, the Browns managed just one winning season from 1990 until 1995. The new economics of the NFL, with escalating player salaries and expenses, also hampered the Browns, who were reportedly losing millions of dollars each season. There was no way to stem the losses without a new stadium. This began the chain of events that took the team from Cleveland to Baltimore.

Members of the Maryland Stadium Authority had spoken with Modell about moving the team to Baltimore, where he would enjoy a publicly funded stadium and a generous lease agreement that would make the Browns profitable again. News of the potential move eventually leaked, and Modell was pressed to comment. Years earlier, he had promised the Browns would never leave the city of Cleveland, but on November 4, 1995, he admitted the landscape had changed. "As far as my proclamation that I would not move the team, that's gone. That's null and void because the game has changed considerably," Modell said in a front-page story in the Cleveland *Plain Dealer*. "We've suffered enormous losses in the last four years." With those statements, the Browns once-inconceivable move to Baltimore now appeared inevitable.

On November 6, 1995, the Cleveland Browns announced they would relocate to Baltimore to play in a new $200-million stadium funded by tax-exempt bonds and lottery funds that would also include 108 private suites and 7,500 club seats. The Browns would play in Memorial Stadium for two years while the new stadium was being completed. The announcement sent shockwaves across the NFL. While state officials and citizens of Baltimore were ecstatic to have the NFL back, the people in Cleveland were shocked and angry. Modell appeared morose as he listened to a speech by Maryland Gov. Parris Glendening lauding the move. Modell was empathetic to a city he called home for five decades but would never be able to even visit again. On November 7, 1995, Cleveland voters approved funding to remodel Cleveland Stadium, but it was simply too late.

"This has been a very, very tough road for my family and for me," Modell said at a news conference in Baltimore to announce the move. "I leave Cleveland after 35 years, and leave a good part of my heart and soul there. I can never forget the kindness of the people of Cleveland, the fans that supported the Browns for years. But frankly it came down to a single proposition: I had no choice."

What followed was a string of lawsuits and overwhelming criticism for the move. Nonetheless, Baltimore had a team again and it was not going to let go. There was some guilt about how the Browns moved. Baltimore felt the same heartbreak when the Colts left. However, the citizens of Maryland were not shown nearly the same amount of sympathy. The Browns players were forced to play out the season in front of a bunch of fans that had to deal with the reality of their team leaving and no longer having NFL football on Sunday afternoons. On December 17, 1995, the Browns earned a 26–10 victory over the Cincinnati Bengals in their final game in Cleveland. It was a heart-wrenching affair for the fans and many of the players.

Once the season was over, the NFL, the Ravens, and Cleveland officials worked to find some type of common ground to soften the impact of the move. A settlement was reached to keep the Browns' legacy in Cleveland, including the franchise's records, logo, and overall history. The NFL would also help Cleveland build a new football-specific stadium with a loan. A new version of the Browns—via expansion or the relocation of an existing franchise—would begin play in 1999. The new team in Baltimore would essentially be an expansion franchise but retain all of the players and personnel from the former Browns to begin play in 1996. The deal pacified all sides. "I am happy for the people of Cleveland. I am happy for the people of Baltimore, and I am happy most of all for the Modell family," Modell said "It has been a long siege, and I am happy it is almost over."

This set the final stage for a new NFL team in Baltimore, where Modell was lauded as a hero. Modell not only moved the team to Baltimore, he also packed up his personal life to settle in Maryland. From there, his contributions went well beyond the football field and he was embraced by the Baltimore community. Modell donated millions of dollars to various charities, including a boarding school for disadvantaged youth and Johns Hopkins Hospital. He was honored numerous times by several organizations and was presented with the Generous Heart Award from the Dr. Ben Carson Scholarship Foundation, which is given annually for excellence in the community.

The Ravens struggled on the field when they first arrived in Baltimore, but they were always active in the community. Players were often seen at schools or other events. In 1998, Modell finally got the new stadium he was never able to secure in Cleveland. Two years later, he won his first Super Bowl. In 2004, Modell capped his 38-year career as the owner of a professional football franchise by selling the Ravens to Steve Bisciotti for more than $600 million. Modell was one of 15 finalists for the Canton NFL Hall of Fame in 2001 and a semifinalist seven times. However, he was never given entry mainly because of the vocal opposition in Cleveland, which has never been fully able to get over the move.

"I think that part of my legacy is I left the colors, the name, and the records in Cleveland," Modell once said about the move. "The fans in Cleveland were loyal and supportive. They lived and died with me every Sunday for 35 years."

Even though he sold the team, Modell remained a familiar figure around the Ravens facility. He often spent time talking to players and coaches. Modell's wife, Patricia, died in 2011. Modell died the following year on September 6 from natural causes. The Ravens dedicated the 2012 season to him and wore a decal on their helmets that simply said "Art." Ozzie Newsome was with Modell throughout his NFL career as a player, coach, and eventually general manager. He was shaken at a Ravens press conference announcing Modell's death as the team prepared to play the Cincinnati Bengals.

"When you think back, as I have over the past 24 hours, of the impact of Art, I can't express it in words," Newsome said. "But based on all the texts, all the emails and all the phone calls I've gotten from people, the impact not only that he had in my life, he had a major impact in their life, too. I just want to end by saying he was a great, great man. Thank you."

It was fitting that the game against the Bengals was scheduled for *Monday Night Football*. Modell was a main force behind the league's rise atop the television ratings each year. On a day full of sorrow, the thought of Modell looking down from Heaven to watch his team play on prime time brought a smile to many of the coaches and players.

"It's an amazing twist. I would say a providential irony, you know?" Harbaugh said. "Maybe they are laughing about that up there right now. Art Modell is a giant. He did pioneer *Monday Night Football*. He was the forerunner of football on TV. That was his vision. Everything that's been done in the league, that's made this America's sport over the last 60 years or so, is because of Art Modell and what he's done. He's a huge part of that—others, of course, too. But Art's a forerunner of that. He's a forerunner of equity—gender and race equity [and] opportunity, a forerunner of that. He loved everybody. He loved players. He loved coaches. He modeled a leadership style that is kind of unheard of and still is. He was a servant leader."

Ray Lewis also paid tribute to Modell, who stood by his side during the controversial murder trial. Lewis said Modell treated him like a son from the first day they met in 1996. Lewis' favorite memory of Modell was shortly after Super Bowl XXXV when the owner performed the linebacker's signature dance on the stage with the Lombardi Trophy. Prior to the Bengals game, Lewis took several minutes to honor Modell before a horde of media.

"Anytime you lose a father, a leader the way he was, to not just his kids, but to many men, it's always hard, because the greatest thing that life offers is the opportunity to really help someone," Lewis said. "He was one of those guys. He was one of those spirits. It's funny, because we are human, and we have real emotions. So it's emotional. It's emotional to lose somebody that the only reason I am in Baltimore is because of him. The only reason the Ravens have a team is because of him.

"The only reason a lot of sacrifices that have happened throughout this league is because of him. Anytime that you can leave a legacy like that, we shouldn't mourn. We do, but we should be celebrating him because he was one of the most awesome men I have ever met in my life. For me to know him, I knew the guy had a real plan. For me to even meet a man like that, with all the impact he had on this world...it's hard losing someone that powerful with that much influence. But one day, we all have to go. So hopefully we send him out the right way with a great celebration."

Modell had two adopted sons, John and David, the latter of whom passed away in 2016. His legacy will always be remembered by the league. Mostly, he will be forever revered in Baltimore for healing the wounds from the Colts' departure and bringing the city championships with the Ravens.

"Art Modell's leadership was an important part of the NFL's success during the league's explosive growth during the 1960s and beyond," NFL commissioner Roger Goodell posted on Twitter when Modell passed away. "Art was a visionary who understood the critical role that mass viewing of NFL games on broadcast television could play in growing the NFL."

STAN'S SIDEBAR

ON ART MODELL

Art Modell was in survival mode. There was no way he wanted to leave Cleveland. He had invested his whole life into Cleveland, the Cleveland Clinic—he was so highly involved with the Cleveland Clinic. When I first heard that, and all my relatives had season tickets to the Browns, I said, "There's no way. That'd be the last team I think would leave, the Cleveland Browns." But Art was not one of these über-rich owners who had billions of dollars. He lived off of his franchise, and he was actually too kind to Cleveland, taking over the stadium, taking over all the financial responsibilities for that, and it just all caught up with him when they built a new stadium for the Indians.

He didn't have a tenant anymore for the old stadium. Then, they built the arena for the Cavaliers. And they didn't do anything for Art. They didn't because they felt Art would never leave. They overplayed their hand greatly, and it cost them. What'd they do as soon as they lost the Browns? They built a stadium. It's the same thing Baltimore did; it's the same thing St. Louis did. If these cities would learn. Oakland's going through it—San Diego, too. So they're going to lose their teams and then they'll probably build their stadiums and try to get a team back. Art was a historical figure in the NFL.

The Colts and the Browns and the Steelers were the ones that went into the AFC during the merger, so there was a lot in common. Cleveland and Baltimore are similar cities, and they respected the name of Art Modell and what he did to his franchise. It was something that they could feel comfortable with. I think they knew if he left Cleveland, he had to be desperate. He's not the type of guy who's just going to come in here and take your money and leave.

Modell made himself part of the community in Baltimore because he had done that in Cleveland, and I think that was sort of his life's mission—the football team and the community. And he knew to grow the football team he needed to be involved in the community. He's the one who reached out to the old Colts, and he knew a lot of them because he competed against them all those years in Cleveland. And they knew him because he was always on the Owners Committee when they negotiated with the Players Association, so there were a lot of relationships there that he was able to build off of.

I talked to him the night before the press conference. I had his home phone because he used to go on Sportsline on WBAL Radio, so when I heard this rumor that there was going to be a press conference and the Browns were actually going to move, I called him. He said, "I can't confirm that, but I'll see you in Baltimore tomorrow." From what I heard, he never set foot back in Cleveland again after the press conference. It had to be a sad day. He was throwing away his whole personal life at that point. All his friends were in Cleveland, all of his business associates were there, all his philanthropy was there. The Cleveland Clinic—I know he hated leaving the Cleveland Clinic behind. He loved the Cleveland Clinic. It wouldn't have happened except that it was either he felt he was going broke and everything he'd done for his family would be gone, or he had to move and he could provide for them very well.

CHAPTER 10
STEVE BISCIOTTI

Steve Bisciotti fully understood the impact of the Colts leaving Baltimore. He had grown up in nearby Severna Park, Maryland, and went to Colts and Orioles games as a child with his father. His knowledge of how a professional sports franchise is ingrained into a community helped his management of the Ravens when he took over as owner in 2004. Bisciotti wasted almost no time putting his stamp on the club.

"My responsibilities are not only to my family and the people who work for the Ravens," Bisciotti said about owning the team. "There are over a million stakeholders in the Baltimore area who we have an obligation to. They're the fans who invest more than three hours on Sunday to watch, listen to, or attend our games. That's a big difference from owning a non-sports company."

More so than knowing football, Bisciotti knows how to build a successful business. Shortly after graduating from Salisbury University, a small school on the eastern shore of Maryland, Bisciotti and his cousin, Jim Davis, started a staffing firm called Aerotek geared toward professionals interested in temporary work in the aerospace and technology industries.

The business was launched in the basement of Bisciotti's home. The firm steadily grew from a grassroots operation to one of the largest staffing firms in the United States, working with engineers, cable installers, computer programmers, marketing specialists, and other professionals. Aerotek eventually changed its name to the Allegis Group, which now has offices throughout the world with more than 100,000 contract employees.

That success helped Bisciotti buy the Ravens, where he has maintained a philosophy of consistent success. One of the first orders of business for Bisciotti as the Ravens owner was providing the franchise with a first-class practice facility. When the Ravens came to Baltimore, they practiced in the outdated facility formerly used by the Colts. In 2004, the Ravens opened a new 200,000—square—foot training center with a brick and stone exterior that became known as "The Castle." The facility includes a 90,000-square-foot fieldhouse with a strength-training area and a full-size indoor practice field. There are also outdoor practice fields spread over 32 acres in Owings Mills, Maryland.

Players can spend their entire day on the practice grounds. In addition to football-related areas, the facility also houses a full-service kitchen, cafeteria, player support functions, basketball and racquetball courts, and a TV studio. "Everything a team needs to help it prepare to win is available to us. Steve [Bisciotti] delivered a first-class, state-of-the-art training facility and office complex," Newsome said. On June 8, 2012, the Ravens reached an agreement with Baltimore-based Under Armour for a 10-year agreement and the Castle officially became the Under Armour Performance Center. It was another shrewd move by Bisciotti to further boost the synergy of the team with the local business community.

"I love the Under Armour brand and am proud that it is Baltimore-based," Bisciotti said. "They started with football wear that players wanted, and still do. They produce great products. Under Armour is the only partner for our training center. Their success has been off the charts, and this partnership will serve as a long-term platform that will showcase to the nation the best of what two of Baltimore's strongest companies have to offer."

While Bisciotti has kept the Ravens financially stable, the team has also performed well on the field under his ownership. Baltimore is one of just five teams to qualify for at least six postseason berths from 2008 to '16. Over that span, the Ravens won at least one game in each of those playoff years and have put together 10 postseason victories—the best mark in the league. With that success, however, Bisciotti has been forced to make some tough decisions.

Bisciotti inherited Billick when he took over the team from Modell. After winning the Super Bowl in 2000, Billick had an uneven performance as the head coach and failed to get the offense rolling. After Baltimore finished 6–10 in 2005, Billick was officially on the hot seat when Bisciotti publicly scolded him during the season-ending press conference, saying the coach "had under-achieved." Bisciotti also intimated that Billick had to be less arrogant and take a stronger approach with the players. As a result, Bisciotti showed the organization and fans that mediocrity was not acceptable.

Billick bounced back the following season with a 13–3 record, but the Ravens took another step back in 2007 with a 5–11 finish. Billick could not overcome that setback and the coach, along with his entire staff, was fired. Bisciotti said it was a difficult decision but one that had to be made. He was simply doing what was best for the organization.

"In order to be successful you have to take chances, and in order to take chances you have to listen to your heart," Bisciotti said in a press conference to announce the firing. "You have to go with your gut. It doesn't mean that you don't fear being wrong, because I do fear being wrong. I could be three coaches past Brian Billick nine years from now trying to solve this puzzle."

Bisciotti also lauded Billick for his contributions to the team. It was the type of balance that savvy businessman try to maintain when publicly discussing a significant change in management. Bisciotti also made sure he took responsibility for the Ravens' recent disappointing seasons.

Accountability went a long way in reassuring the fan base that the team was dedicated to getting back on top. Despite the recent shortcomings, Billick would always be a huge part of the Ravens franchise, leading the team to their first Super Bowl victory.

"How much blame you put on different people, and how much you hold yourself responsible, is new to me," Bisciotti said. "I hope that over time that Baltimore views me as [good] an owner as Brian Billick was a head football coach. I've got some catching up to do to the man that I asked to step down today. The jury's out on me. Brian's already got his Super Bowl."

The firing of Billick meant Bisciotti had to make another tough decision—hiring the next head coach of the Baltimore Ravens. The challenge of finding the best candidate was critical to the future of the franchise. Bisciotti and the front office took the most direct route in trying to hire Cowboys offensive coordinator Jason Garrett, who later decided to stay in Dallas. From there, Bisciotti thought outside the box and brought in Eagles special teams coach John Harbaugh, who impressed the Ravens from the first moment he met with them. While some fans were underwhelmed by the eventual hire, Bisciotti knew he had made the correct decision.

"We all saw something in John. And you have to be willing to separate yourself from the masses—take some chances—to achieve great success," Bisciotti says. "There's probably a little bit more perception that we took a risk with John. We don't think we did."

The move certainly paid off. Harbaugh delivered a Super Bowl in 2012 and has become one of the league's top coaches. While the Ravens have experienced highs and lows during Bisciotti's ownership, the team has always been regarded as a model franchise. The team has maintained one of the best fan experiences at the downtown stadium with huge tailgate areas. The scoreboards and video inside the stadium have been upgraded. The team's practice facility is one of the best in the league and is open to fans during training camp. The Ravens recently moved forward with renovations to the complex to allow more fans to interact with the team during preseason.

Bisciotti generally addresses the media once per year. This meeting occurs at the end of each season, unless, of course, another pressing issue emerges. Bisciotti is always direct and forthcoming with the press on issues related to the Ravens or the NFL. When Baltimore missed the playoffs for the third time in four years in 2016, Bisciotti was asked whether he was worried about empty seats during regular season games or disgruntled fans.

"I'm always concerned. I said apathy is the worst emotion, in the past," Bisciotti said. "There's a lot more disappointment and anger than apathy, so I don't think we're at any kind of critical stage there. The fact that our renewals have always—good times and bad, even back in the '04, '05, '06, '07 era—our renewals are kind of always in the 97.5 to 98, 99 percent [area]. We have other people willing to buy those PSLs and come in. We've kind of been through the same slump.... Let's face it, you talk about people moving out of town and people divorcing and giving up their tickets. We've never seen the fluctuations based on our success."

Bisciotti continued: "I still, to this day, can't understand how somebody that has a PSL and has tickets that doesn't go to two of the games doesn't give them to their neighbor, neighbors' kids or their babysitter or somebody else who is dying to go to those game. But it happens. People wait until the last minute and decide they're not going to go. It's disappointing, but to me, they should be prepared for an opportunity to make somebody else happy that doesn't go. I don't really think they're not going because they're protesting. I think maybe the more we lose, the more they get distracted by other things, and we lose that priority on a Sunday. It's obviously significant; I just don't know how much it fluctuates."

One thing is clear—Bisciotti maintains his vision for the Baltimore Ravens. The goal is to add a few more Lombardi Trophies to their collection. Bisciotti is confident he has the staff in place to meet that goal. While some fans called for change after the 2016 season, Bisciotti was confident the best course of action was to maintain consistency. Bumps in the road are inevitable. Consistent change can be a recipe for disaster.

"I did not get to where I was by just firing people," Bisciotti said. "I think it is a bad model, especially in this business. But I do not have as much to fall back on, except then saying, 'Trust me, this is the right way to run a business.' That is not good enough for probably a quarter of our fans. They are like, 'Then you are over the hill, and you are an idiot!' That is fine with me. I would be more than happy to take some blame for that if that is what they consider to be my weakness."

STAN'S SIDEBAR

ON STEVE BISCIOTTI

Once Art Modell got here, he had built up their estate tax issues and all these different ideas on how to structure things if he died, because he only bought the team for a couple million dollars, and the value was here. They had to restructure it in a way, and they needed an investor. I think Ron Shapiro put them all together and came up with the idea that Steve would let Art still own the team for a certain number of years.

Art knew how old he was, and then Steve would have the right to purchase the rest of the team. It was a deal that Art probably didn't want to make, but it was a deal that he had to make because he made the move so he'd have all these financial resources to pass on to his kids and his family. He could have survived, but there wouldn't have been as much income to pass down to generations, which is what he wanted. He wanted to leave that as his legacy. And this was the way it could be done without the government getting all the taxes.

Steve obviously grew up as a Colts fan. He has pictures of himself with Johnny Unitas and Lenny Moore as a kid up at training camp. I remember I used to own health clubs right across the street from his business, and he'd be over there working out every day, and this is right when he started his business. He grew that thing into a monster. He provided employees for the new technologies that were coming on—permanent and temporary. It started off just being temporary employees that he would train and then send into these companies, and it grew from there. He grew that; he was in the right place at the right time. Then this team became available. He had the money. He loves football. It was just a natural fit for him, and a natural fit for what Art needed to do. I think Steve stayed in the background early and wanted to learn. He's a smart guy. He didn't want to step in there, out of his element and not be successful.

This gave Steve a chance to become accustomed to the way the business was run, the way the NFL was run. It was the perfect fit, and I think that's the only reason it happened, the only reason that Art sold at that point. Steve was the buyer because it was the perfect fit for both of them. I think he's done great as an owner. I think he hires good people, lets them do the job, but he's involved. He loves getting involved. By any stretch, you don't see his car there very often during the season. But he's on the phone with John almost every day.

Steve is an involved owner, but not a micromanager. He wants to know what's going on, he'll give an opinion, but he's not going to make people do it the way he wants to do it—like he said recently, he trusts his partners. He trusts Dick Cass, he trusts Ozzie Newsome, he trusts John Harbaugh. Now, he has opinions. Sometimes they're right, sometimes they're wrong, but he has his opinions and he'll voice them but he's not going to demand that his opinions rule the day every day.

They've had good ownership from Art Modell to Steve Bisciotti. I think that's the key. They've been very accountable with their people. They've been willing to give you the resources to get done what you need to get done. Steve Bisciotti has done that, from building the Castle to improving on the stadium, all those different things it takes to maintain your position in the league, and he's hired good people and been able to keep good people, like Ozzie Newsome, through this whole stretch. Being able to keep Eric DeCosta, even though he's had been multiple offers from other teams to be their general manager. You keep good people. Kevin Byrne has been in PR for all these years. He's sort of the face of the Ravens to the media.

You get a professional like that, and you look good to the media. So all these things factor into the success of a franchise. You've got to get great coaching They've had Brian Billick and they've had John Harbaugh, and they've both won a Super Bowl. They've both been to the playoffs multiple times. John comes from a great football background, and he has a philosophy that he keeps, and I think everybody in the organization buys into that philosophy of tough, physical, hard-nosed football. You play the kicking game. You play defense, and you win most of your games that way. They've had Joe Flacco the last nine years. You've got to have a quarterback.

Ozzie keeps saying he's not going to retire as long as Joe's still there. You need that quarterback, and he's been able to win football games, which is the only statistic you need to judge a quarterback. So all those things factor into why they've been able to maintain and be consistent and be like the Patriots and the Steelers and the good organizations that are always there, not the ones that get in for a year and then don't make it for five years, and then get in for a year and don't make it for five more years. You win the game during the week by preparing. You become a great franchise with everything you do behind the scenes in preparing for the draft, in preparing for free agency and preparing for things that might come up that you don't expect, preparing the team for that last two minutes of a game, for the last 14 seconds of a game. They practice all the different scenarios so they know what to do when they get into those situations. That's the key for being successful, not just preparing but preparing in such a way that you can take that preparation to the game. That's the reason I felt I played all those years is I knew I couldn't keep up with guys like Tony Dorsett and O.J. Simpson. As I said, my theory was to find out where they're going and go over there and wait for them. Because I wasn't going to run with them. You've got to be a step or two ahead of people in this league to be successful. Harbaugh is big on preparation; every scenario is practiced from replay to time-outs to all those situations. Not that you never make a mistake, because you do. A lot of times you do what you prepare for and it doesn't work, so people think it's a mistake to do it that way. It's always results-oriented. If you run a fake punt, and all of a sudden the guy trips coming out and it doesn't work, people say, "Oh, that was a horrible call." But if he'd have done it the way you prepared to do it, it would have been a great call.

A lot of judgements are results-oriented. The Ravens do this every year consistently. It doesn't change from their end-of-season "State of the Ravens" press conference to their meetings in Florida to their preparation for the draft. They stay the course. The only time they didn't do that was after the first Super Bowl. They decided to invest a lot of money trying to win a second Super Bowl, and it didn't work and it set them back for a couple of years. I think they learned from that to stay the course. They signed a bunch of the guys to try one more time to get one more Super Bowl out of it, and then Jamal Lewis got hurt and Elvis Grbac came in and wasn't successful. It just didn't work out, and they paid the price for several years.

CHAPTER 11
ED REED

The Baltimore Ravens were able to grab Ed Reed with the 24th overall pick in the 2002 NFL Draft. Reed was a consensus first-team All-American selection as a senior at the University of Miami and was named the *Football News* National Player of the Year. Despite those accolades, there was not much hype around the undersized Reed when he was drafted. Baltimore reportedly had set its sights on Boston College running back William Green, Arizona State offensive tackle Levi Jones, and Northwestern linebacker Napoleon Harris. But all of those players were gone by the time the Ravens were on the board. All Reed did was become one of the greatest safeties in the history of the NFL.

"The thing that really sold me on him is every time we watched Miami's defense and they needed a play to be made, Ed Reed made that play," Newsome said after the selection. "When they needed a fire to be put out, Ed Reed put the fire out."

Reed amazed coaches and players with his ball-hawking skills as soon as he stepped onto the field. There was no question he was going to be an impact player. On September 30, 2002, the entire nation got a true sense of Reed's talent when he recorded his first interception and blocked a punt in a 34–23 victory over Denver on *Monday Night Football*.

Reed started all 16 games as a rookie, finishing fourth on the team with 86 tackles (69 solo). He tied the Ravens rookie record with five interceptions, which also led the team that season. Reed earned the franchise's first two blocked punts, one of which was returned for a touchdown. Just as with Ogden and Lewis, the Ravens knew they had a special player on their roster capable of doing great things on the football field.

The momentum carried over to 2003 when Reed earned a Pro Bowl bid in just his second year. Reed tied a then-franchise record with seven interceptions and blocked two more punts. He was the main difference in several games. For example, in a November 23 game against the Seattle Seahawks, Reed blocked a punt and then returned it 16 yards for a touchdown. That sparked one of the greatest comebacks of that season. The Ravens trailed by as many as 17 before tying the game with 10 points in the final two minutes en route to a 44–41 wild victory in overtime.

Earlier that season, against the Arizona Cardinals, Reed was named Special Teams Player of the Week when he blocked a punt and returned it 22 yards for a touchdown.

Reed not only gave the Ravens a boost each game, he was a model of consistency. He mostly avoided serious injuries and was a mainstay in the starting lineup. Furthermore, he affected the way opposing teams would game plan. They simply tried to stay away from his side of the field. Not only could Reed break up passes or intercept quarterbacks, he was capable of running the ball back down the field 80 yards. The risk simply outweighed the reward to challenge him.

In 2004, Reed was further recognized for his prowess on the field when he was named the Associated Press 2004 Defensive Player of the Year. Reed was the first safety in 20 years to take home the honor. Seattle's Kenny Easley has been the most recent safety to win the award in 1984. Reed led the NFL and set a Ravens franchise record with nine interceptions. In just his third season, Reed had sole possession of Baltimore's all-time interception record. He also broke the NFL single-season record with 358 interception return yards.

"A lot of great players have truly achieved this award, and I'm just in my third year," Reed said. "I love football. I just want to have fun with it, and whatever else comes with it, comes with it."

Reed was a staple on NFL highlight shows throughout his career. There was just no telling what he could do. On November 7, 2004, against the Cleveland Browns, Reed set another NFL record with a 106-yard interception return for a touchdown. That score, with 45 seconds remaining, sealed a 27–13 victory and earned Reed the AFC Defensive Player of the Week.

"It's really just exciting for me to go out and play the game, to get up on another Sunday and have the same kind of fun you've been having since you were a kid," Reed said. "That's just me. It's really just me enjoying the game for what it is. To know that I can make a play, or maybe even win the game—that's exciting to me."

Reed also was gaining the attention of former all-time greats, who recognized that he was on his way to a potential Hall-of-Fame career. "I played with Tim McDonald, a Pro Bowler, Mert Hanks, tremendous safety, Darren Woodson, and none of them compare with Ed Reed," Deion Sanders told ESPN. "The guy's tremendous, by far. He should win the Player of the Year. What else does he have to do?"

In 2005 Reed was hampered by a high ankle injury, which forced him to miss six games. He still finished with 40 tackles, 12 passes defended, and one interception. Baltimore finished 6–10 without him in the lineup consistently. However, that was the last lackluster season of his storied career. After the shortened season, Reed was named to the next five consecutive Pro Bowls for the Ravens. He just never appeared to slow down.

In 2008, Reed led the NFL again with nine interceptions that he returned for 264 yards and two touchdowns. On November 23, he broke another NFL record by returning an interception against the Philadelphia Eagles 107 yards for a touchdown. He flapped his arms like a bird as he reached the end zone, setting off a raucous celebration at M&T Bank Stadium. Reed's jersey and the football were sent to the Pro Football Hall of Fame.

"Ed has been doing that for a long time in his career, and [it's] probably the first time this year where he's had one of those kinds of games where he basically takes over the football game," Ravens coach John Harbaugh said in his Monday press conference the day after the game. It was fun to watch, me being here for the first time, to see it firsthand. I know what you guys have been watching all these years. And then he's done it through the injuries. He rehabs really hard."

Reed continued to be a fan favorite and led the charge at a pep rally attended by thousands at the Inner Harbor prior to Super Bowl XLVII. However, that championship marked the end of Reed's time in Baltimore. He became a free agent at the end of that season, and the Ravens opted not to resign him. Reed later inked a deal with the Houston Texans, but a long career had taken a toll on his body and performance. After being released by Houston on November 12, 2013, Reed reunited with his former defensive coordinator in Baltimore, Rex Ryan, who was then the head coach of the New York Jets. He sparked the Jets with three interceptions over seven games. At the end of the season, Reed knew that was the end of the road.

While he had not officially retired, Reed sat out the 2014 season. He was ready to play if a team needed him, but the call never arrived. On May 7, 2015, Reed, who was 36, returned "home" and signed a one-day contract with the Ravens. The team held a formal press conference for the announcement, and Reed was surrounded by former teammates and coaches who bade farewell to one of the all-time greats. Reed was later inducted into the franchise's Ring of Honor on November 22 of that year.

"I'm really appreciative of the Ravens family," Reed said. "From day one when Ozzie first called me and asked me if I was ready—he just said, 'Are you ready?'—and I told him, 'Yes.' And then I came in that next day, my hair all over my head, and he has Ms. Val [Wideman] braid my hair back there. But I'm very appreciative of the Modell family [and] Steve Bisciotti. [There are] so many people I want to thank [for] supporting me, from Little League all the way up to being in the NFL, so many people that helped me get to this point. Even [having] the success here with the Ravens, so many people helped me."

Newsome lauded Reed's ball-hawking skills. The general manager remembered watching tape of Reed at the University of Miami and marveled at his game-changing ability. When there was a critical moment for the Miami defense, Reed always seemed to make the play to either get the ball back to the offense or even secure a win. Newsome also marveled at the easy transition Reed was able to make from college to the NFL.

"I had the privilege of watching him play, and I know every time pre-snap, the quarterback wanted to know where Ed Reed was," Newsome said. "Every time post-snap, they better know where Ed Reed was, because he would make the pick or make the play that we would need."

Harbaugh remembered the speeches Reed gave to his younger teammates about Baltimore and what the Ravens meant to the community. Harbaugh admitted he got goosebumps watching videos prior to the press conference of Reed making countless plays. However, Harbaugh said Reed's talents were not just based on natural ability. He said Reed spent hours watching film to uncover a quarterback's nuances or how teams ran particular plays. The extra work paid off. When the Ravens needed a big play or spark, Reed often delivered a decisive blow to the opposition. "I'm just proud to be around him, be associated with him, and be able to call him a friend," Harbaugh said.

The Ravens may never see another player like Reed, whose accolades include: seven-time Pro Bowler (2003–04 and 2006–10), Associated Press NFL Defensive Player of the Year (2004), The Sporting News All-Decade Team (2000s), and *USA Today* All-Decade Team (2000s). But Reed's contributions went beyond the football field. Each home game throughout his career, he provided tickets to children in need. He also helped launch fitness programs and football leagues for schools in Baltimore City. On that warm spring day in May, Reed's career had come full circle—the place where he signed his first and last NFL contract.

"This is where it started, and I knew this is where it was going to end," said Reed, who is eligible for the Pro Football Hall of Fame in 2020. "Home is here. Home has always been in Baltimore. My heart has always been in Baltimore. It will always be in Baltimore and M&T Bank Stadium."

STAN'S SIDEBAR

ON ED REED

Ed Reed is the Deion Sanders of safeties who are more than willing to gamble. They may be completely out of their responsibility, but they'll make a big play out of it. Every once in a while, they'll give up a big play. People scheme to get them to guess, and sometimes that happens.

It happened with Sanders, but quarterbacks hate to play against that because they never know where you're going to be. They always want to know where everybody is so they can make their reads, but you never knew where Ed was going to be. You never knew when Sanders was going to undercut a pattern or if he was going to jump a route. He might have had a man, and he may completely jump off his man and take the underneath pattern at the last second. As my coach always told me, if you guess, you better be right. But it was always an educated guess because, like with Ray Lewis, Reed had film study. So he knew when to guess, and he was willing to take chances.

You saw what he did after he intercepted passes, often lateraling the ball; sometimes that was crazy, and those were not always great things to do, but that was his personality. You didn't want to rein him in, because you wanted him making those plays.

Ed Reed was just a guy who knew when and where and how to make a big play. When I played there was a guy named Paul Krause. Ed was like him on coverage but 10 times better than him against the run. Krause wouldn't even try to hit anybody. He

144

would just not become part of the physical aspect of the game at all. Ed would go up and hit you. He could hit you, he could blitz, and he could make plays on special teams. He could block punts, and he could return kicks. Krause could never do any of those things. But he intercepted a lot of passes because he knew where to go and where to be, and Ed was like that.

CHAPTER 12
THE DRAFT

Ozzie Newsome is widely regarded as one of the top personnel executives in the NFL. He was a Hall-of-Fame tight end for the Cleveland Browns before taking coaching positions and moving into the front office after his retirement. In 2002, he became the NFL's first African American general manager. Newsome helped put together Baltimore's Super Bowl XXXV and Super Bowl XLVII championship teams.

he Ravens have been able to build much of their success through the NFL Draft. The team has drafted several future Hall of Famers in the first round and has found unlikely gems later in the draft. From its inaugural draft in 1996 when it landed Jonathan Ogden and Ray Lewis, Baltimore has become a model for other NFL teams on how to build a solid foundation for long-term success thanks to Newsome, assistant general manager Eric DeCosta, director of college scouting Joe Hortiz, and senior personnel assistant George Kokinis.

With the Ravens' success over the years, the team has not had the luxury of picking early in the first round. From 2001 until 2016, Baltimore has only picked in the top 10 of the NFL Draft twice—choosing Suggs with the 10th overall pick in 2003 and offensive lineman Ronnie Stanley with the sixth overall selection in 2016. Over that span, the Ravens have picked 20th or higher 11 times. As a result, the scouting department needed to be meticulous with its assessment of players who could make an impact in the NFL. The Ravens have mostly succeeded, but they did have a few misses.

"From '96 to 2004, we drafted three Hall of Famers [Jonathan Ogden, Ray Lewis, Ed Reed].... When you're picking in the Top 10 of the draft, you have a chance to be a lot more successful than when you're picking anywhere from 20 to 32, which [are] the positions we've been in," Newsome said prior to the 2015 NFL Draft. "Unfortunately, we lost 11 games [in 2015]. Now we're back in the Top 10 again. But I would say [the season] was not up to my standards, was not up to Eric's standards and not the Ravens' standard when you compare [it] to what we did very early on."

The Ravens have managed to grab some key playmakers late in the first round. Baltimore grabbed tight end Todd Heap with the 31st overall pick in 2001. Over 10 seasons, Heap caught 467 passes for 5,492 yards with 41 touchdowns—the best among all tight ends in franchise history. The following season, Baltimore took Reed with the 24th overall pick, and he became one of the best defensive players in NFL history. Other notable players grabbed late in the first round include offensive tackle Michael Oher (No. 23 in 2009), cornerback Jimmy Smith (No. 27 in 2011), and wide receiver Breshad Perriman (No. 26 in 2015).

However, the Ravens also had some uneven performances in the first round. Mark Clayton was taken with the 22nd overall selection in 2005 and never became the go-to receiver the Ravens had envisioned. Still, Clayton's numbers were respectable over his five years with the team, catching 234 passes for 3,116 yards with 12 touchdowns. Safety Matt Elam, taken with the 32nd overall pick in 2013, struggled with injuries and consistency. Offensive lineman Ben Grubbs (29th overall pick in 2007) and Oher left for bigger paydays with other teams and never fully left their mark in Baltimore.

"I think what we've learned over 20 years is what not to look for," Newsome said. "If you take a receiver, do you go with just production? Sometimes production is not the answer. If you take a quarterback, do you just go with arm strength? Sometimes that's not the answer. And if you take a running back, he's good with the ball in his hands, but he can't pass protect. I think what we've learned over the years is what *not* to look for, rather than what to look for."

Baltimore, however, has been largely successful finding gems in the later rounds. That is one of the reasons Newsome likes to accumulate picks. The Ravens staff has also been able to find solid undrafted free agents who eventually become starters. This ability to uncover these unheralded players has been the foundation for the team's success. Baltimore also lets players leave via free agency if they think the contract is too expensive. This allows the team to pick up extra draft picks when these free agents leave the team. These compensatory selections are determined by the NFL Management Council using a formula based on salary, playing time, and postseason honors. Some of the players the Ravens drafted through this process became vital contributors, including Pro Bowl fullback Kyle Juszczyk, right tackle Rick Wagner, Pro Bowl punter Sam Koch, offensive guard Edwin Mulitalo, and quarterback Troy Smith, who won the Heisman Trophy at Ohio State.

In 2016, the Ravens had 11 selections in the NFL Draft, including five picks in the fourth round. Of those 11 players, six made an immediate impact that season. Stanley has shown he can become a longtime fixture at left tackle. Another offensive lineman, Alex Smith, who was taken in the fourth round, also appears to be a longtime starter and can play on both sides of the line.

Another fourth–round pick, Tavon Young, emerged as the Ravens' best cornerback when Jimmy Smith went down with back and ankle injuries. Running back Kenneth Dixon, the final fourth-round pick, showed he could carry the load as the starter. Harbaugh knew shortly after the draft the team had acquired some solid playmakers.

"I just want to mention the great job that our scouts do—Ozzie, Eric, Joe—and the leadership that they display. It was flying in the room," Harbaugh said. "The bullets were flying; it was moving fast, early. It was moving fast when we had those back-to-back picks, and we had trades going on. Pat [Moriarty, senior vice president of football administration] was hard at work with his calculator, trying to pound away the numbers. Just watching these men, and the way they work in the heat of battle, under fire, was really something to behold. I wish everybody had a chance to see it. It was just phenomenal the job that our staff did—[that] our scouting staff did, led by Ozzie—to operate the board the way they did."

Even when the draft is completed, the Ravens are still working the phones and bringing in players who were not selected but have the potential to make an impact. Baltimore gives these undrafted players a fair opportunity to make the team, as opposed to just using them for extra bodies in training camp. As a result, Baltimore has become a desirable place for these undrafted players to sign. Baltimore enjoyed its most success with this strategy at linebacker.

Bart Scott, who was undrafted out of Southern Illinois in 2002, was one of the most heralded free-agent signings. He initially made his mark on special teams and eventually became a starting linebacker. Scott made the Pro Bowl in 2006. Other notable undrafted players are Jameel McClain, Dannell Ellerbe, and Albert McClellan.

"We've had a lot of success with the undrafted college free agents," Newsome said. "What we'll do is we'll be prepared when that opportunity comes to be able to still try to get in the mix and hopefully come away with some guys that could be productive players for us."

Another key signing was Zachary Orr, who signed with the team in 2014 after going undrafted out of North Texas. Orr, like

Scott, made an early mark on special teams before getting increasingly more time at linebacker. He eventually became one of the stars of the defense. Orr knew he had talent but also needed an opportunity. Baltimore was the best landing spot to show that he could play in the NFL.

"It definitely gave me an edge. When I got here, I couldn't have come into a better situation, with so many undrafted guys on the team and hearing from those guys," Orr said. "One thing Albert told me was, 'You'll always be undrafted.' No matter what you do, that will always follow you."

Orr had a breakout year in 2016. He was a vocal leader of the defense and tied for eighth in the NFL with 132 combined tackles. Orr also earned second-team All-Pro honors. However, Orr's career was cut short when he was diagnosed with a congenital neck and spine condition during a physical after the season. That condition leaves him more vulnerable to paralysis or even death if he continues to play. Orr had no choice but to retire at the age of 24.

"One thing that helps me be at peace with this is I gave it my all," Orr said at a press conference to announce his retirement. "I don't have any regrets, on the field, off the field. I can leave with a lot of stuff, but one thing I can't live with is regret. I don't have any of that in my body."

Players like Orr embody the spirit of the Ravens. The draft is always an exciting time for the team because it provides hope and opportunity. Baltimore maintains a solid personnel staff, which is often offered opportunities from other teams. Some stay and some decide to take the promotion. The Ravens, however, have managed to stay astute, finding quality young players from all levels of the college ranks. That prowess will remain a hallmark of the franchise.

"It seems like everybody is very much on the same page about the type of team that we want to put together," Harbaugh said.

STAN'S SIDEBAR

ON THE DRAFT

The Ravens need to do the things that they've been doing and remain consistent. I think they will do that. You know, everybody's saying, "John Harbaugh's on the hot seat." I don't think so. I think Steve Bisciotti has a lot of confidence in Harbaugh. John wants to be the coach here for 20 to 25 years. He's been here for 10 years now, and he wants to be like Bill Belichick. He wants to be like Don Shula, like those coaches who stayed in one place and had a great, long, successful run. I think he's going to do it here because he's got the backing of both Ozzie Newsome and Steve Bisciotti, the guys he directly reports to.

You still have to make the right decisions at the right time. They have got to hit in the draft. They haven't always hit in the draft, but I think if you look at each one of the drafts, none of them is really bad. Sometimes they got better players in the fourth and fifth rounds than they did in the first and second round.

I don't see any reason to make major changes at this point. I think Joe Flacco's going to have a really good year in 2017, one year removed from that knee surgery. I think it really affected his play in 2016. He won't admit that. He may not even know that it did, but I think it did because I've been through it. I finally threw the brace off and said, "The hell with it. I've just got to go out and play." Once I did that, I was effective again.

Joe's been through that now, and I think he's going to say, 'The heck with it,' and go out there and play. To me, it was stepping into the throws. Watch Tom Brady; he had that horrible knee injury that he had to come back from and [he had to] learn to step back into those throws. The telling thing for me was when I interviewed Joe after a game, and he really did step into a throw and fit it in between three defenders.

I remember saying to him, "Joe, I saw that throw. You really stepped into that one. What was the difference?" And he said, "I just said, 'The heck with it.' I was just going to throw it in there." And that's what he did. I think he's got to take that attitude on every play. You have to get over the mental part of it.

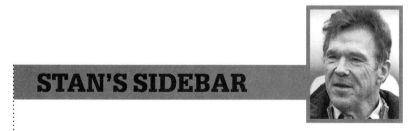

STAN'S SIDEBAR

ON THE 2016 SEASON

I had high hopes for 2016. I thought going in the Ravens could be 7–0 going into the bye week. I thought they needed to be 5–2, and if they were 4–3 or less, it was going to be a battle. They ended up 3–4. They easily could have been 5–2, and those games came back to haunt them. The loss against the Jets, that was a horrible loss. They were a horrible team. Even the game here against Oakland, they should have won that game. They needed 10 more yards, and they dropped two passes and they didn't get it. The way Tucker kicked this year, that would have been a win.

October was a horrible stretch, especially the Washington game, when Breshad Perriman caught the winning touchdown but didn't get his feet down in the end zone. I thought John Harbaugh did a great job of re-grouping them during the bye, coming back and beating Pittsburgh, and then later going to Pittsburgh on Christmas Day with the opportunity to still make the playoffs. If you started the season, you'd have said, "Okay, if we're playing Pittsburgh on Christmas Day to win the division and make the playoffs, we'll take that right now." And they got back to that point despite that horrible four-game losing streak.

It took a lot to get there. That's why you saw what you saw against Cincinnati. Everything, all the air had been let out of the balloon. If they hold Pittsburgh one yard short and win that game, then they destroy Cincinnati in that game. They'd kill Cincinnati. The Bengals wouldn't have won. But football is an emotional game. If you don't have an emotional edge, what you saw in Cincinnati happens—and it did.

CHAPTER 13
MATT STOVER

Kicker Matt Stover was a model of consistency for the Ravens. Stover, who retired in 2009, finished with 2,004 career points (fourth all-time in the NFL). He also made 471 career field-goal attempts (fourth all-time in the NFL), including an NFL-record 445 FGAs outdoors. He made the Pro Bowl in 2000 and holds the NFL record for consecutive games with a field goal—38 from 1999 to 2001.

The word is *consistent*. That's the best piece of language available when trying to describe the kicking skills of Matt Stover. On a team loaded with flashy players who were often in and/or demanded the limelight, Stover proved to be a bit different. The shadows suited him just fine. He had the mind-set of many good kickers—"I'm just here to do my job".

And Stover did it very well. He started his career slowly, staying on injured reserve with the New York Giants—the year they won the Super Bowl—in 1990. New York signed Matt Bahr, who kept the job the rest of the season and forced Stover to remain on the sideline. The Cleveland Browns signed him as what was then called a Plan B free agent the following season, and he began kicking with them.

Stover stayed with the Browns until the team moved to Baltimore in 1996. Then, when the team went on its wild run to the Super Bowl in the 2000 season, Stover played a huge role. He hit on 35-of-39 field goals, something that proved to be crucial as the offense struggled mightily throughout various stretches of that season. The offense, in fact, went through a five-game stretch where it could not score a touchdown. Simply put, the Ravens lived off of Stover's field goals for nearly one-third of the season.

But that year the Ravens were fortunate because they fielded arguably one of the greatest defenses of all time. Stover finished the season with 135 points—a career best for him—and came up with a number of crucial kicks. In fact, at the press conference where he announced his retirement, Stover remembered how the defense delivered a message to him and the offense about all they needed from them against the Giants in that Super Bowl.

"The defense called out the offense and they said, 'You get us 10, we win. That's 10 points. All we need is 10,'" Stover said at his retirement press conference. "To an offense, that's pretty cool."

The Ravens scored first when quarterback Trent Dilfer threw a touchdown pass to Brandon Stokley, and Stover added the PAT. With that 7–0 lead, Stover then nailed a 47-yard field goal late in the second quarter. The offense gave the defense its 10 points, and then some. Final score: Ravens 34, Giants 7.

"When I'm trotting out on to the field, I hear from Rob Burnett, 'We get 10, we win, Stove,'" the kicker said at the retirement conference. "I said, 'Gee, thanks for the extra pressure, man.' We got the 10 points, and we were in the locker room at halftime, and they said, 'We got it. It's over.' And it was. It was over. So that was the most memorable kick that I ever had."

He certainly came through with enough memorable kicks. In the end, Stover became the team's all-time leading scorer with 1,464 points. He kicked for the Ravens from the time the team moved to Baltimore in 1996 until the team decided to part ways with him after 2008. Still, Stover got one more shot at the big time, signing with the Colts in an ironic twist the next year after kicker Adam Vinatieri was injured. The Colts went to the Super Bowl that year, where the Saints upset them. Stover retired after that, ending his 19-season NFL career.

But even that season had some of Stover's style on it. There was no question that Stover had the consistency few NFL kickers ever did. It's a reason why he played on three teams that made it to the Super Bowl (including that Giants team the year he did not play). In fact, an ESPN.com article on February 2, 2010, published just before the Super Bowl where the Colts took on the Saints, poked a bit of fun at how long Stover had been in the game.

In that article, Stover mentioned that he watched that famed Giants-Bills battle on the sidelines with injured quarterback Phil Simms and musician Jon Bon Jovi. The kicker also said that he wore his Giants Super Bowl ring on the plane while the Colts flew to the Super Bowl.

"Some of the guys were like, 'Whoa, I was like three years old when you got that," Stover said in the article.

The sad part of that game for Stover was that he missed a field goal early in the fourth quarter. This game, expected by many to be a Colts rout, didn't turn out that way. The Saints stayed close, and thanks to a great game from quarterback Drew Brees and a gutsy onside kick call from coach Sean Payton, New Orleans was able to score 15 points in the fourth quarter and pull out a 31–17 victory.

The Colts called upon Stover to try a 51-yard field goal early in the fourth quarter while clinging to a 17–16 lead. Now, as Stover's career went on, his problems with longer kicks intensified, but this was a tough situation for the 42-year-old kicker. He missed the kick, and the Saints bounced back to win the game. Since New Orleans scored two touchdowns, the missed kick didn't kill the Colts. The main thing it did was deny them a four-point lead.

Kickers always have to prove themselves. It's the nature of the job, much like a pitcher in baseball. You just have to keep showing that you can do this, because there are so many other guys waiting to take that job. That's just a way of life for kickers—especially in the National Football League, another subject Stover touched on when saying good-bye.

"Well, you really have to re-prove yourself every year. Ozzie will tell you that," Stover said. "As a player, it's not what you've done, it's what you're going to do, because you need to understand that it's a very competitive environment. But the competitive nature of me was, 'I'm never going to let a guy beat me.' And I never did let a guy beat me."

However, Stover was tested when new coach Brian Billick took over in 1999. As noted, Stover's long-range kicks were not his strong point. Overall, Stover went just 13-for-32 in kicks of 50-plus yards throughout his career. During Billick's first season, Stover missed several kicks early, including a few long ones. That concerned Billick, and the Ravens brought in some other kickers to look at. Stover said much of the trouble came due to a "communication breakdown" between Billick and Stover and their special teams coach. The problem was resolved, and Stover proceeded to finish the season 18-for-18 after that. He signed a new contract and had his big year in 2000 as the Ravens won the Super Bowl.

"We've all seen me have some bad days," Stover said. "It's what you do with that and those lessons that you learn from poor performance in order to get better. And I always let the misses teach me a lot more than the makes. [In 1999], I had to communicate with Brian. We did, and we got it worked out. I hit 18 straight field goals, and then we signed a new contract and kicked it into the Super Bowl, if you remember, right? Brian learned a lot through it, he told me. I learned a lot through it. It made me a better kicker."

Stover became more consistent as time went on, slipping a slight bit in the later years, although he was still a solid kicker. But Stover's contract expired after the 2008 season, and Baltimore did not re-sign him. He got some feelers from other teams during 2009 before the Colts picked him up mid-season after Adam Vinatieri's injury. That's when they made the Super Bowl, and Stover ended his career in a bit of style.

In the end, Stover kicked just one season for John Harbaugh, who made his mark as an NFL assistant coach by often working with special teams. Harbaugh, however, enjoyed having Stover, not only as a good kicker who could still get the job done at his age, but as a player the new coach could turn to for some help with locker-room situations.

"As a first-time head coach…being able to go to Matt, have him come up to the office, grab him on the field, grab him in the locker room or whatever, and ask him what he thought, and what he thought we needed to do and what direction we were going—that was invaluable," Harbaugh said at the retirement press conference. "That's without the kicking part of it. That's the kind of leader he is. I know he's been that way his whole career, but that year was huge just for me personally."

Stover's longtime consistency remains with the fans in Baltimore even though he last kicked for the team in 2008.

When Billy Cundiff missed the field goal that would have sent the game into overtime in the famed playoff game in New England in 2011, some radio talk show callers and people on the Internet were saying things like, "Stover wouldn't have missed that." And now that Justin Tucker has grown into one of the NFL's top kickers of his day, people still compare him to Stover at times.

The main similarity between the two is that consistency. The lone kick that Tucker missed in 2016 was blocked. So he was never wide left, wide right, or short. Kicking has changed in the NFL since Stover left the game after 2009. Long-distance kicking has become thought of as much less of a risk, and many more kickers can blast field goals from more than 50 yards. In fact, they do it all the time. Tucker has already tried 40 kicks of more than 50 yards—and made 28 of them, going 10-for-10 from long-range in 2016—in just his first five years. Stover, as mentioned earlier, tried only 32 kicks from more than 50 yards in his entire career.

In the retirement press conference, Newsome mentioned the fact that the issues with longer kicks and shorter kick-offs were talked about at times. Still, Stover got through and became a kicker the Ravens depended on for a very long time.

"Not only was he reliable, he was very competitive," said team GM Ozzie Newsome at that press conference.

STAN'S SIDEBAR

ON KICKING

The Ravens had the luxury of having, if not the best, one or two of the best kickers in the league for most of their existence between Matt Stover and Justin Tucker. You know, the kicking game is so underrated. Good coaches know that the kicking game and special teams are really one-third of the game because of field position.

Jim Tressel, former coach at Ohio State, used to say that the punt was the most important play in the football game.

If you get it blocked, it changes the whole momentum of the game. You return one for a touchdown, it changes the whole momentum of the game. If you pin a team back inside its own 5-yard line, that can change the whole momentum of the game.

The kicker position is vastly underrated, and to have a guy like Stover is great. In the game then, it was about what you do 40 yards and under. Now it's what you do 50 yards and under. And if you can add icing to the cake and do 50 yards and over, it's great. Matt wasn't great from beyond 50, but I remember he kicked one to win a game in Cleveland beyond 50. When you had to win a game, you'd want Matt Stover out there to win. "Money Matt" is what former Raven and former broadcaster Rob Burnett always called him. He was always money. I don't remember him ever missing a game-winning kick. People complain about your kickoffs and all those different things, but Matt Stover was one of the best kickers that ever played the game. He won a lot of games. And then in the Super Bowl year, Matt was winning games—a little like Justin Tucker did in 2016. The Ravens didn't score a touchdown for five straight games. He kept them in contention.

Their defense and their kicker catapulted them into the Super Bowl, which, by that time, their offense started going too, in the playoffs. Matt's a guy of strong faith; he's big in the community. When he moved here, he never anticipated living here, the same way I didn't when we moved here. I always assumed I'd go back to Ohio when I was done. But then you get here, you get in the community, you start to raise your kids here, they go to schools here, and you become part of the fabric of Baltimore. I think that's what happened with him. He used to go back to Texas between seasons, and then all of a sudden, he started staying here and having kids and stuff. He got more and more involved in the community, and he had more and more success on the field, and it was good for both parties. It's hard to be a kicker and a leader.

He definitely was a leader in the community for the franchise, and he was a leader of the special teams group; there's no doubt about that. It's tough for a kicker to lead when you've got guys like Ray Lewis. But Matt was on the players' committee that went in with Brian Billick and set up a lot of the rules and so forth, so as far as kickers go, Matt was probably one of the guys who showed the most leadership of any kickers who have played the game.

CHAPTER 14
THE 2000 SUPER BOWL RUN

Many expected the Baltimore Ravens to make their first run at the playoffs heading into the 2000 season. It made a lot of sense. Second-year coach Brian Billick had given the team a lift in his first year the season before. They went from three losing years under first coach Ted Marchibroda to 8–8 under Billick in 1999—and they looked much more competitive while doing it.

In addition, the team's young defense really seemed to be growing and coming together. Led by young linebackers like Ray Lewis, Peter Boulware, and Jamie Sharper, the Ravens were becoming harder and harder to run—or throw—against because the group featured so much quickness and speed.

The offense, however, became a different story. It stumbled badly midway through the season under starter Tony Banks, and Billick pulled the plug on him in the eighth game, putting in backup Trent Dilfer. That move didn't inspire a lot of confidence among Baltimore fans, as Dilfer had been considered a bust with Tampa Bay.

The Ravens didn't do much better on offense in Dilfer's first start, a 9–6 loss to the Steelers at home. That added to the complaining from fans—and for an interesting reason. Baltimore now had gone five games without scoring a touchdown. Yet still the team was staying in the playoff hunt with a 5–4 record through the first nine games. At some point, the touchdown slump would have to end.

Billick made it clear that the Dilfer move was not going to be reversed. Banks had a good arm, yet a penchant for interceptions at the wrong time seemed to come with it. Billick wanted to make a change.

Jamie Sharper was part of the group of young linebackers that quickly transformed the Ravens defense into the most feared in the NFL. He combined with Ray Lewis and Peter Boulware to give the Ravens a group that covered the field from side to side every game. They were a big reason the Ravens became one of the best defenses of all time in 2000 en route to winning the Super Bowl title.

"Clearly, we have got to do something to change the impetus," Billick said in an AP story on October 23, the day he made the change. "Trent brings certain aspects to the offense—his experience, a certain tempo that we can benefit by. And he's been down this road before."

Dilfer had been benched by Tampa Bay the previous season and became a free agent in the offseason. The Ravens signed him, and Dilfer started the season as a backup. That's when Billick made his move.

"One of the biggest things about this position is you have to prepare to deal with failure," Dilfer said in that same article. "Tony [Banks] has handled it like a total pro. He can't let this setback affect him too negatively, the same way I didn't let my setback last year affect me."

Dilfer remained the quarterback the rest of the way for Baltimore—and with good reason. The Ravens took off from there and won their final seven games. The offense scored 193 points in those games, averaging more than 27 per contest.

Overall, Dilfer's numbers were not great, but they were good enough. He completed 134-of-226 for 1,502 yards. He threw 12 touchdowns but also tossed 11 interceptions. Somehow, though, Dilfer found a way to make the right plays at the right times a few times each game. He wanted to come to Baltimore and hoped that it would be a place where he could finally find his way and become the kind of quarterback he always wanted to be.

Those were the things that Dilfer thought about while rattling around on the backup quarterback market after the 1999 season. The decision as to where he'd go next had to be defined by a few things.

"I was going to a place where I could develop my skills, become a better player, and prove to people that Tampa wasn't me," he said on an NFL Network video. "I never doubted that I'd be the quarterback for [the Ravens]."

And when Billick gave him the job, Dilfer, after the initial loss, got off to a pretty good start. The Ravens scored a big victory over the Bengals—ending the five-game streak without a touchdown—and then edged Tennessee, Dallas, and Cleveland. Dilfer helped the offense ring up 122 points with nine touchdown passes and just four interceptions. After that, though, he began to sag.

In the final three games, still all Baltimore victories, Dilfer totaled three touchdowns and five interceptions. In the playoffs, the offense began having more problems, and some of the initial criticism of Dilfer started coming on again. The first playoff game came at home against Denver, and that's where the football gods began shining on the Ravens and Dilfer once more.

First of all, Denver's backup quarterback, Gus Frerotte—best known for head-butting a wall during his days with the Redskins and knocking himself woozy—started the game due to injury issues for starter Brian Griese and didn't play great against the ferocious Baltimore defense. Still, the offense wasn't moving well, and the Ravens needed a bit of luck to take command of the game late in the second quarter.

Dilfer threw a short pass to the right that bounced off some Denver defensive players and into the arms of Shannon Sharpe, who quickly turned it into a 58-yard touchdown that gave the Ravens a 14–3 lead. They went on to win 21–3 and move on to the AFC divisional game at Tennessee—a game that seemed like a tough victory, even though the Ravens had pulled out a one-point victory there during the regular season.

This time, a blocked field goal from Keith Washington turned into a 90-yard return for a touchdown by Anthony Mitchell in the fourth quarter. That snapped a 10–10 tie and put the Ravens in front for good. Ray Lewis then added another touchdown with a 50-yard interception return for a score and that, combined with some key missed field goals from Al Del Greco, gave the Ravens a stunning 24–10 victory.

That game saw Dilfer complete only five passes in 16 attempts for 117 yards. But it also pushed the Ravens into the AFC championship, another road contest, this time in Oakland. Once more, Dilfer's numbers did not blow anyone away—9-for-18 for 190 yards. However, just about half of them came on one drive that helped change the game for good early in the second period.

The Ravens were backed up and facing a third-and-long from their own 4-yard line in a scoreless contest. But Sharpe stepped up once more. He ran a slant pattern, Dilfer nailed him over the middle with a quick pass, and the tight end took off. He went the distance for a stunning 96-yard touchdown that gave Baltimore a 7–0 lead. That's a typical scenario in the playoffs. The offense would move the ball just enough to do a little bit of damage, and then Dilfer would make a play, often with Sharpe. This time, the quarterback liked the matchup he saw, and everything paid off.

"I like any safety on Shannon Sharpe, and I was actually supposed to work the other way," Dilfer said in an article in the following day's *Baltimore Sun*. "He made a break and we hit it. He just did the rest."

Shannon Sharpe played for the Ravens for just two years (2000–01) but became a big team leader and helped them win a Super Bowl and also make a playoff appearance. Sharpe made some big plays in the 2000 postseason en route to the championship, the biggest being touchdown catches versus Denver and Oakland. The tight end gave a struggling passing attack the kind of target it so badly needed.

Some of the Ravens also had some fun with the fact that it seemed to be taking Sharpe a bit of time to get to the end zone. In the final yards of his journey, wide receiver Patrick Johnson actually caught up to the tight end.

"I consider myself pretty fast, but it was like, 'I'm slow. I'm taking a long time to get to the end zone," Sharpe said in an article in the following day's *Chicago Tribune*. "I didn't realize it was that far. It seemed like I never got to the end zone.... Patrick Johnson scared me because he almost tripped me twice."

The defense did the rest of the work that day, intercepting four passes and recovering one fumble. A Duane Starks interception set up a Matt Stover field goal later in the quarter for a 10–0 halftime lead. Oakland stayed within one score thanks to a third-quarter field goal, but Stover added two more kicks for the 16–3 final.

The defense held the Raiders to 191 total yards. Quarterback Rich Gannon was injured, although he tried to play through the pain. Oakland just could not get going against the Baltimore defense, which was playing its best football of the season at the right time. They believed they were tough to beat.

And they were.

"The confidence that we had was a belief that we had," backup linebacker Brad Jackson said. "There's no question that each week everybody was going to do their jobs. Our confidence was high. We weren't arrogant. We were confident. We were dominating—and a lot of that started with Brian Billick. His only rule was if you talk it, go out there and back it up."

Now came the Super Bowl. The Ravens came into the AFC playoffs as the No. 4 seed out of six teams and were considered by many to be a surprise. Up next were the New York Giants, the NFC's top seed, coming in after a rather easy 41–0 victory over the Minnesota Vikings in the conference championship game.

But they were no match for the Ravens in the Super Bowl. The song remained the same for Baltimore—vicious defense and just enough help from offense and special teams to help the Ravens earn a 34–7 victory and the team's first Super Bowl title. The franchise—formerly located in Cleveland—had last won a championship in 1964, beating the Baltimore Colts in that year's title game.

Dilfer again did not post numbers for the ages. He completed 12-of-25 passes for 153 yards and one touchdown. However, the Ravens scored once on a Starks interception return, once more on a Jermaine Lewis kickoff return, again when Jamal Lewis ran for a touchdown, plus two Stover field goals.

The defense made all that stand up—and more. Some players on the defense told Stover before the game that if the offense could score 10 points, they'd win the game. It turns out they were right on target. Still, heading into the game, the offense—especially Dilfer—was taking a lot of heat for performing so inconsistently, with many people also saying the defense was simply carrying Baltimore to its success that season.

"I was getting a lot of heat," Dilfer said in an NFL Network video later on. "There was a lot of criticism on [being] the worst quarterback ever to go to the Super Bowl. Now I had a chip on my shoulder. It's supposed to be about winning, not glamour."

That's what the Ravens made it about—winning. The entire Ray Lewis incident from the previous year was brought up often,

Jermaine Lewis was a local guy who made good with the Ravens for a while. He came from nearby Prince George's County, played at Maryland, and became a dynamic kick-return specialist with the Ravens. He sometimes helped at wide receiver, too. Lewis scored a crucial touchdown on a kickoff return in Super Bowl XXXV.

and Billick drew national attention when he basically told the national media to leave Lewis alone because that matter had been taken care of. That took a lot of heat off of Lewis, who went out and played a spectacular game, finishing with five tackles, four passes knocked down, and a good job in pass coverage. He was all over the place, tormenting New York quarterback Kerry Collins in so many ways but especially when Baltimore blitzed.

Dilfer put the Ravens in front with a 38-yard touchdown pass to Brandon Stokley midway through the first quarter. Stover added a field goal late in the second period for a 10–0 halftime lead. The Ravens increased that when Starks returned an interception for a 49-yard touchdown in the third quarter.

The Giants scored on the next play thanks to a Ron Dixon 97-yard kickoff return. But the Ravens slammed the door when Jermaine Lewis answered with an 84-yard kickoff return for a touchdown on the play after that. Baltimore now held a 24–7 lead, and the Giants never scored again.

Dilfer said that he and the offense just kind of shrugged off the criticism coming into the game. They had to have heard it—after all, it was coming from many different places—but the quarterback said they decided to take a different path.

"We just decided as a group that winning, that looking each other in the eyes, was more important than what you guys say about it," Dilfer told the media.

One of the most satisfying things for Dilfer had to be the fact that the game was played in Tampa Bay, the city that let him leave just one season before. Interestingly enough, even though the city of Baltimore went crazy after the victory, the Ravens were facing a decision about what to do at quarterback.

They did not bring back either Dilfer or Banks. Instead, they signed Elvis Grbac, who had problems throughout 2001 and, by season's end, was essentially playing the game manager role that Dilfer had the year before. In fact, Grbac retired after that season, never playing again.

That entire situation proved very frustrating to Dilfer because, even though his statistics were not spectacular, the Ravens went 11–1 with him at the helm and won a Super Bowl. It's a question that the team and Dilfer had to address many times over the years. How can a quarterback win the championship yet not be good enough to play for you the following season? It's a question that still comes up in Baltimore to this day, especially because it took the team until 2008—when it drafted Joe Flacco—to create a stable situation at quarterback.

The Ravens repeatedly said that it was a very tough decision. It was easy to see that they did not want to talk badly about Dilfer, especially after he'd just helped them win a Super Bowl. Still, the problem was that there were other free-agent quarterbacks out there who could throw better and probably generate more offense than Dilfer. That was something the Ravens needed the following year, as they lost starting running back Jamal Lewis and offensive lineman Leon Searcy before the season even began. Still, that team made the playoffs in 2001, even winning a road game before losing at Pittsburgh.

Billick, talking to the *Baltimore Sun* in a Q&A in 2010, said that it was an organizational decision.

"It's my job to represent that decision, but this was not me waking up one day and saying, 'You know what, we need a new quarterback,'" Billick said in that article. "This was done over a month-long period of time, like you do every position. Trent was one of several free agents, so we had to consider we might lose Trent to another team. What's out there and can be better and what's available? It would be a bold step, but clearly, what we did offensively had to be better. To think we were going to repeat the all-time greatest scoring defense in the history of the game was to ask a lot of our defense.... We came back individually and saw it the same way—[we] created the collective plan [that] this is how we go about doing it. The consequence was Elvis Grbac."

STAN'S SIDEBAR

ON THE FIRST SUPER BOWL TEAM'S DEFENSE

It's hard to be better on defense than the '70s Steelers defense, which has Hall of Famers like Mel Blount, Jack Lambert, Jack Ham, Mean Joe Greene. They were pretty dominant, and they did it for a decade. But it's harder to keep a team together these days than it was when the Steelers were there. Back then there was no free agency. You didn't lose players. You built for a generation. You built for a decade.

The 2000 defense, they had great players. Marvin Lewis did a great job of using the players. It wasn't very complicated. They didn't do a lot of stuff. He stayed real basic, but they had great linebackers. They had those two big tackles up front. Rob

Burnett and Mike McCrary were rushing on the outside, Rod Woodson in the secondary. Their corners were good enough; one of them was great—Chris McAlister. Duane Starks had a great year. McAlister was a lockdown corner at that point, and you need one of those guys. You need one of your corners to be a lockdown corner to let him take the best guy. The linebackers, especially Peter Boulware and Ray Lewis, they were really, really good. They were a very confident bunch, and they went onto the field and did it.

They were not the number one ranked defense in the league that year. They were number one in points. Probably for that one season, they were the best, although the Steelers had one year that they were very dominant, too. I think they had four straight shutouts, and when Terry Bradshaw got hurt, the defense took over and didn't let anybody score. It's almost like Dick Butkus and Ray Lewis. I can't separate them. But those are the top two I've ever seen. Being a defensive player, it was great to watch them because they didn't have to trick you. A lot of times, defenses want to trick you with all these exotic blitzes and different things. They didn't have to do that. They could just stay basic and say, "You know what we're doing, but we're going to beat you anyhow."

If you can do that defensively, if you can rush four guys and drop the seven, you're way ahead of the game. The Ravens didn't run a lot of exotic blitzes. They ran a 4–3, and then Boulware sometimes would go down as a defensive lineman when they went to their nickel, and they took a defensive lineman out, and he would be a pass rusher from a three-point stance. They didn't do a whole lot of different personnel groups. They didn't do a whole lot of stunts and stuff. They did them but that's not what made them great.

It wasn't the scheme that made them great. They had a really good scheme based on who they were, but they were just really good players at their positions, and they didn't care if you knew what they were going to do. They would just beat you.

CHAPTER 15
JUSTIN TUCKER

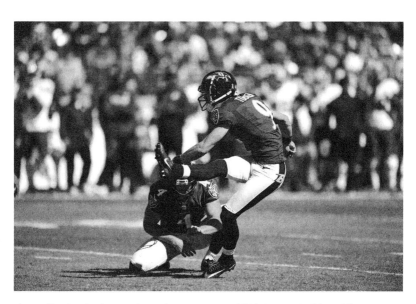

Justin Tucker had a nearly perfect season in 2016. He made 38-of-39 field goal attempts—the lone miss coming on a block in New England where the player came leaping over the line of scrimmage—and earned a spot in the Pro Bowl. The undrafted free agent has grown into one of the NFL's top kickers.

Justin Tucker's career with the Baltimore Ravens sort of began while he was still in college at Texas in late 2011.

Billy Cundiff served as Baltimore's kicker that season and, after making the Pro Bowl in 2010, struggled at times in 2011. He began missing most of the long-distance kicks the Ravens asked him to make. That caught the attention of fans and team personnel.

There were some worries about Cundiff's increasing inconsistency. The Ravens were clearly among the top teams in football, and the best teams need consistent kickers. That topic came up more as Cundiff began having more problems, and those problems became more noticeable in the AFC Championship Game at New England in January 2012.

The Patriots were clinging to a 23–20 lead in the final minute when Lee Evans could not hold on to a Joe Flacco pass that would have given Baltimore the lead—and likely the win. A stunning play, Evans had the ball for a brief moment in the corner of the end zone but could not hold on, and that brought out Cundiff. However, he badly shanked a 32-yard field goal attempt, pulling the ball far left, which ended the Ravens' season and sent the Patriots to the Super Bowl.

After that, the Ravens signed Tucker, who was not selected in the 2012 draft. He raised a few eyebrows during his early offseason work with the team after his strong career at Texas. People wondered if the rookie was truly challenging the veteran Cundiff. That proved to be the case as Baltimore cut the incumbent during the preseason, giving Tucker the job.

"To the naked eye, it doesn't look like I've made a lot of changes, but I've made a complete transformation from the kicker I was in college to the kicker I am today," Tucker said in an ESPN article that week. "I feel like I'm kicking the best I ever kicked."

The move paid off handsomely. Tucker played a big role in 2012 when the Ravens surprised many with a late-season run that ended with a Super Bowl championship, helped by the rookie kicker and a number of tough playoff kicks.

In his first season, Tucker went 30-for-33 on field goals—including making all four attempts from at least 50 yards. Longtime kicker Matt Stover's Achilles heel was the long kicks, although he was good for anything inside of 50 yards throughout his long career with the franchise.

Tucker's initial season also included big postseason kicks, the best of which came in double overtime on a brutally cold day in Denver. Like the well-known cat, the Ravens found nine lives that day, and Tucker clinched the 38–35 victory with a 47-yard field goal. Two games later, Tucker made two field goals in Baltimore's 34–31 victory over the 49ers in the Super Bowl. Overall, he went 4-for-4 in the postseason, helping the Ravens become World Champions.

Tucker's successes continued the next three years. He made 92.7 percent of his 2013 kicks and 85.3 of them the following season. Tucker converted 82.5 percent of his field goal tries in 2015 despite having some trouble with longer kicks. But all of that changed in 2016.

Tucker's best year overall came in 2016, even though the Ravens did not make the playoffs. He was picked for a second Pro Bowl after turning in a nearly perfect season—and one of the best an NFL kicker ever produced. In fact, one could make the argument that no kicker ever fared better in one season because, quite frankly, he almost never missed. He made 38-of-39 kicks plus all 25 of his extra-point attempts. In addition, Tucker made all 10 of his attempts from 50 yards or longer. Plus, 22 of Tucker's 33 field goals from that season were from 40 yards or longer.

He made 35 straight field goals before his lone miss of the season, a blocked attempt against the Patriots later in the season. That became the fifth-longest streak of all time in the NFL.

"I am very fortunate to work directly with true professionals on a daily basis. Morgan Cox is the best snapper in football, and Sam Koch is the best punter and holder in football," Tucker said in a statement. "We believe in working hard, we believe in each other, and we care deeply about becoming the best football players we can be."

Tucker got the most notice thanks to all of the long-distance kicks he made in 2016. And that came after the aforementioned struggles with that area in the previous two seasons.

In 2015, Tucker connected on just 4-of-10 from at least 50 yards. The previous season, the kicker made only 4-of-9 before everything changed in 2016.

His teammates love to tease the kicker throughout the season, especially since Tucker is different than other players. Kickers always get a bit of a different treatment from teammates since they're not out there tackling and blocking and going through the physical drills that others do.

Tucker always gives that credit to Koch and Cox for helping him do his job. The kicker brings plenty of confidence to the field every time the Ravens play, but the "Wolf Pack," what

Tucker calls that group of three, has helped him become arguably the top kicker in the NFL. And he never hesitates to give them the credit.

"To me, it is imperative to have a quality long snapper and a quality holder before you worry about how good your kicker is," Tucker said in 2016. "You have to have the first two steps before the ball leaves anybody's foot, and those two are the best in the business. To be able to work with those guys, to be able to learn from each other over these last [five] years, has been awesome, and knowing that we are going to be able to keep going and hopefully make ourselves some of the longer-tenured specialists...I think that the opportunity to do that is a very good deal."

One of Tucker's biggest moments of 2016 came when Baltimore edged the Bengals 19–14 in a late-season game. The Ravens needed help from their kicker in 2016, much as they did from Stover while contending for the Super Bowl in 2000, because the offense was not consistent enough and struggled getting the ball into the end zone. This day belonged mostly to Tucker, who nailed three field goals of more than 50 yards—connecting on kicks from 52, 54, and 57 yards—all in the first half. In fact, the two longer kicks came in the final two minutes of the second quarter and proved crucial in giving the Ravens a big victory.

The Ravens had a lot of fun teasing Tucker after the game. He's quite an outgoing person, and when asked about the kicker, linebacker Terrell Suggs laughed, shook his head, and said that the kid "would love this," as the veteran prepared to unleash a stream of compliments about Tucker.

"We've got the best kicker in the league," Suggs said. "There's no doubt about it. But we've got to keep the young kid humble. Like I said, I told him when I [came] back [from an injury], I've never seen a kicker make some contract demands, but I guess when you're the best kicker in the league, you can do that. It's great to have, like I said before, a kicker with ice in his veins."

Making three field goals of more than 50 yards is not something that happens every day. In fact, Tucker became the first kicker in NFL history to do that in the first half of a game. That's why Suggs was so complimentary.

Others were just shaking their heads after that game. Tucker already had established himself as one of the league's top kickers, but that Cincinnati game really set the tone. In fact, the only kick he missed in 2016 came a few weeks later in New England. That's when linebacker Shea McClellin took a running start and made a flying leap right over snapper Cox's head and blocked Tucker's try at a 34-yard field goal. Tucker truly had no chance as his streak of 35 consecutive field goals ended. That wound up being the only kick he missed all season long.

"That guy's special, that's for sure," offensive lineman Marshal Yanda said the day of the win against Cincinnati. "What he did today, and he's shown it all year long, that guy's in a zone. It's huge. You see teams around the NFL that are struggling with their kickers, and it's nice to have him where he's confident and kicking the ball really well."

The Bengals and others have noticed the way Tucker has grown into such a dangerous offensive weapon.

"Certain kickers can't do what he does," Bengals linebacker Rey Maualuga said after that game. "Sometimes, when it's a

40-plus-yard field goal, teams end up just punting the ball. You do a good job on defense, and the ball is left in his hands. It's more like an automatic three."

Interestingly, there had been some off-the-field tension between Tucker and the Ravens when both sides were talking contract. Tucker finally signed a four-year contract extension (for a reported $16.8 million) right before the deadline to make a deal. That contract means Tucker will be with Baltimore until at least 2019.

"Justin has become a cornerstone for our team," general manger Ozzie Newsome said in a statement about the contract. "What is good for the Ravens right now is that we have our Pro Bowl special teams group—Sam [Koch], Morgan [Cox], and Justin— signed through the next three seasons."

But Tucker's become very well-known in the Baltimore area in a number of ways. He's a true opera singer who performs around the community and often shows up in commercials—something that's a bit unusual for kickers/punters. However, there's no question that he's one of the best-known members of the Ravens since arriving in town in 2012.

Pro football and all sports have changed over the years. Athletes used to be popular if they were stars, like quarterbacks or wide receivers, or had special personalities. Kickers—way back in the day—often were people who played other positions when the rosters were smaller. But there's so much specialization in football nowadays that a kicker has just one job.

Tucker is different because he sports an unusual personality. He's a people person who can sing opera. He's not afraid to give his opinion in many ways, and that's one reason his teammates like him. The Baltimore fans are well aware of who Tucker is and why the commercials keep coming.

The Tucker TV commercials are all over the area. Add that to his amazing singing abilities, and the kicker—the *kicker*—has grown into one of the team's best-known players. That's not something that happens too often in today's NFL. But then again, it's not too often that kickers can make nearly every kick, sing opera, and have a wild personality. The combination is an unusual one, and it's worked well for the Ravens since Tucker joined the team five years ago.

What's happening more and more with Tucker, though, is how people outside of the locker room are getting a good look at his loosey-goosey personality. That's just who he is, and Tucker never hesitates to have some fun. He gave the local media a good look the day he made all of those long field goals in the Cincinnati game. Tucker walked into the post-game press conference and stopped at the podium.

"It smells like updog," Tucker said.

The media folk paused for a moment. Finally, someone asked, "What's updog?"

Tucker then displayed a devilish grin and said, "Nothing much, man. What's up with you?'

The room groaned, Tucker laughed, and many people just shook their heads. That's Justin Tucker.

STAN'S SIDEBAR

ON JUSTIN TUCKER

Jan Stenerud is in the Hall of Fame, and he's supposed to have this big booming kick leg. Beyond 50 yards, he was 25 percent. Justin Tucker is almost 70 percent from beyond 50 yards. I mean, there's probably been no better kicker. He's up there with the best of all time already because of his range and his accuracy. There are very few like that. Matt Stover was very accurate, but he didn't have a great record beyond 50 yards.

It's almost like there's a 10-yard-greater difference in today's game than there used to be. They used to say you don't miss within 40 yards. That's what you wanted. Now you want a guy who never misses within 50 yards. He'll do 70-yarders in warm-ups, if you watch, depending on where the wind is and what day it is. I mean, if they put in that rule where you get one point for putting it through the goal posts on kickoffs, I'm all for it. Why not? He's a guy who will do that 10 or 12 times a year. Kickers don't get drafted very often. That's 'cause you just don't know how they will adjust to the pro game. It's a completely different thing. It used to be because they used a tee in college; they don't use a tee in college any more, so you can get a little better handle on it.

When you're playing for money, and that's all on the line, it's a lot different than when you're in college. There's no doubt about that. Some guys are better playing for money. Some guys are worse playing for money.

Justin Tucker is the best kicker in football, period.

CHAPTER 16
ERIC WEDDLE

During the Ravens' glory years, the defense led the way. They were known as a rough, tough, hard-hitting bunch. The line was nearly impossible to run through, the linebackers were the tough combination of hard-hitters who could cover receivers pretty well, and the defensive backs could shut you down. Not a pretty picture for opposing offenses.

But that's the way the Ravens played for several years, led by players like Ray Lewis, Ed Reed, Terrell Suggs, and others. They rattled your bones when they hit you, and not many offenses loved to go against the Ravens. Unfortunately, the defense struggled a bit after winning the Super Bowl in 2012. Reed was let go, Lewis retired, and Suggs battled some injuries as the defense grew a bit younger and tried to get back on its feet.

Suggs remained a major force on the defense, but the signing of safety Eric Weddle before the 2016 season proved a big boost. Weddle would have been a perfect fit during the defense's glory years in so many ways.

Weddle made the Pro Bowl three times during his 10 years with the San Diego (now Los Angeles) Chargers and amassed a long list of awards. He twice made first-team All-Pro on the Associated Press team (2011, 2014) along with three times on the second team. He was twice named a first-team All-Pro pick on The Sporting News team (2011, 2014). The Chargers named him their Defensive Player of the Year in 2011, 2013, and 2014, and their Most Valuable Player (2012).

That's why Weddle was such a great pickup for the Ravens, who were thrilled to get him before the 2016 season, as noted by coach John Harbaugh.

"To have a player that has done so much over the last 10 years in the National Football League, who we've played against,

[who] we understand what he brings to the table, who knows how to play the coverages already, who knows how to get a back end lined up [is just great]," Harbaugh said. "[Weddle] understands positing, understands disguise, understands pressures—all the things that we won't have to talk about from day one that he brings here and can also help our young guys with. I hate to say [he's] a coach on the field, because the reason we coach is because we can't play. We have a player, though—a great player—that thinks like a coach and that understands the game that way. In the back end, that's really, really valuable."

The Ravens needed that leadership because their secondary had struggled over the past few years, especially in terms of coverage. They played much better at times in 2016 with Weddle back there, but they still had issues. He made four interceptions and 85 tackles plus a sack, which gave a defense that was a mix between young and old a real lift at times.

Weddle talked about that after one of the defense's top efforts of the season, a 38–6 thrashing of a good Miami team on December 4. The safety wound up being the first person to enter the room where the media does post-game interviews with Harbaugh and certain players, and Weddle looked like he was still ready to play.

He walked to the podium and screamed a few times. That caught everyone's attention—and made just about everyone laugh. Weddle then unleashed a torrent of compliments for a defense and a team that seemed to be coming together and had shut down a pretty good opponent.

"What a great game, team effort, all three phases," Weddle said. "We talk about it. I've been talking about it all season, that it's a process. This team's going to fight, scratch. We believe in each other, and we're going to continue to get better, or try to, as the season goes on. Huge, huge confidence builder and playoff football. We've been playing playoff football for the last four weeks, so it's nothing new to us. It's a good team that came in, riding high, and to put on the performance that we did was outstanding and was fun to be a part of."

Weddle also talked about how important it was for him to come up with an interception in that game. He'd dropped balls a few times during the season but said it was important for him to be able to come back and keep fighting

That's the only way to learn in the National Football League, something Weddle felt was crucial for younger players to understand. That's how a leader sets an example.

"Hey, you get humbled. You go back to work, and any time you've struggled, any time you don't play well, you make mistakes, I know only one way," Weddle said. "And that's to work harder and continue to believe in yourself, and you've got a group, this organization, my teammates and coaches, that believe in you.... It makes it easy to move past those not-so-good plays you have and move forward."

That hard work ethic is something that Weddle's Ravens teammates have noticed and appreciated. When Lewis played on the team, his brutal work ethic made teammates shake their heads in awe. There are a lot of similarities between Lewis and Weddle.

Weddle studies hard, practices hard, and plays hard. And he's the type of leader that the Ravens need on defense at this time, because it is made up of a mix between a young group trying to learn and grow and a bunch of veterans who know their way. But leaders are needed on any defense—and offense.

That's why quarterback Joe Flacco spoke up loudly when Weddle initially was not picked for the Pro Bowl—although the safety was later added. Flacco brought up good points that made him sound like he was a defensive teammate of Weddle's.

"There is no doubt [he got snubbed]," Flacco said. "I think Eric's season speaks for itself, just what he has gone out there and done—tackles, interceptions, and all of that stuff. Now, having said that, you do not get a chance to see the kind of leader he is, the type of person [he is]."

Flacco emphasized the importance of Weddle's leadership skills, something that made Weddle so valuable in a season like that. He had to come to a new team, a prospect that probably became tougher since he'd been a major force with the Chargers for 10 years.

Not only did he join the Ravens, Weddle played a major role and quickly grew into a leader after signing a four-year contract. That's not an easy task.

"It is not easy to come to a new team, come in here and try to prove to everybody 'I belong here, I'm a good player,' and at the same time be a leader right away," Flacco said. "That is the thing you can feel from Eric. He has come in here, and he has not been bashful. He made the right impact right away in leading this football team. How he plays on the field, that speaks for itself."

The Ravens will need his impact in the coming years. At deadline time for this book, there were many questions about a Baltimore defense that looked good for much of the 2016 season but faded badly at the end—especially against the running game.

There are going to be younger players who need to step up on the defensive line, at linebacker, and especially in the secondary.

The Ravens have had problems the last few years in pass coverage, really needing to improve there—an issue they've yet to fix on a consistent basis.

But a player like Weddle gives the Ravens a player like a Rod Woodson, who played on their Super Bowl champion team in 2000. He's back there to both make plays and help direct the show. Reed made plays and gambled all over the place. Weddle is a different kind of ballhawk than Reed, who got burned several times while taking chances. That won't happen as much with Weddle, a player the Ravens are going to need to be steadier while their secondary and defense try to come together and grow.

The Ravens also suffered a tough loss at the end of the 2016 season when linebacker Zachary Orr, one of the team's most pleasant surprises of the year, a player who began growing into a real force at his position, suddenly and shockingly announced his retirement at the age of 24 due to a medical condition that showed up after a late-season injury.

One of the players who showed up at the press conference to show their support for Orr was Eric Weddle.

Weddle knew how the team had suffered problems on defense in 2015 during a 5–11 season. One of the big reasons came from a lack of turnovers on defense. Weddle, and the coaches, talked about how much they needed to change that in 2016.

In fact, the Ravens improved in that area, especially in the secondary. They finished with 18 interceptions in 2016—with Weddle tying for the team lead with four, matching linebacker C.J. Mosley. That's a big improvement from 2015, when they made just six interceptions during their injury-riddled season and the secondary was repeatedly torched by opposing quarterbacks.

That's one of the reasons the Miami game meant so much to the Ravens. Baltimore picked off three passes in that game, often downfield, which gave the offense great chances to score, something it needed since the Ravens had their own problems in that part of the game.

"[The turnovers], it's huge," Weddle said. "We know the struggles that happened last year. We work on it. We talk about it. We preach it. Turnovers are the equalizer in any game, and to get there, the pressure...the disguising, and when the plays were there to be made, we made them. And that's huge for us. It's something that we strive to be. We're trying to be the best, each play, each game."

The question now will be where the Ravens go from here in the defensive secondary. They'll face a number of key decisions, because there's no question that players and help are needed. Smith is a strong shutdown corner, but he's gotten hurt throughout his career, and the Ravens truly could use another player back there.

Another question is who can play safety with Weddle. Lardarius Webb shifted over from corner to safety and connected well with Weddle. The question after 2016 was whether or not Webb world be back.

But the Ravens know that Weddle will be back in the second year of a four-year contract. He loves the game too much. Some of the things he said at the press conference when he was introduced to the Baltimore media certainly showed that.

"And for me personally, I'm a simple guy," he said. "I live and breathe football. It's my family away from my family, and

I sacrifice a lot of time with my kids and my wife to give everything I can to my team. The things that Baltimore [will] give me is that—a team that gives everything for each other, a team that wants to win, wants to go back [to the playoffs], has the goal to win a Super Bowl every year."

CHAPTER 17

FOR THE LOVE OF FOOTBALL

The affair that took place between the city and fans of Baltimore when the Colts played in town from 1953 to 1983 was filled with emotion on so many different levels. Baltimore lived and died with the Colts all the time—and that relationship would have exploded in the Internet age. Remember, this was before social media, before everybody knew everything about everyone in sports—and in life. How many levels did this love touch? Well, let's take a look.

The game times were set at 2:00 PM so that churches could have their Sunday sessions and the patrons could then make their way to Memorial Stadium over on 33rd Street. Now the games are at 1:00 PM thanks to television, the ruler of all in sports. The heroes of the Baltimore Colts usually and often did stay to live in the city after their careers ended and often became successful businessmen, revered for years after they last laced up their cleats. They were Colts, and that never changed. They were Colts.

During the three decades the Colts were in town before the Irsays snuck them out in the middle of the night in a snow/ice storm in 1984, they were *it*. They were *the team*. Which, in some ways, could be a bit difficult to understand given the other tenants in town—the Baltimore Orioles.

The Orioles grew into a powerhouse in major league baseball in the 1960s and '70s. They made the World Series in 1966, 1969, 1970, 1971, and then once more in 1979. Plus, they found their way to the American League playoffs in 1973 and 1974 and became contenders in the American League East for first place—that was the only way to make the playoffs back then—every year.

Despite all that success, despite having Hall of Famers like Brooks Robinson, Frank Robinson, Jim Palmer, and manager Earl

Weaver, sadly they weren't the Colts. This was the Colts' town, and they were Baltimore's team. Why? Who knew, exactly? But there's no question that Baltimore became a football town. The city fell passionately in love with the Colts during their first five years of existence, something that really fell into place for good when the team won their first NFL championship in 1958.

That's when the Colts beat the New York Giants 23–17 in overtime at Yankee Stadium on national television. All of the key components were there. First came the cool, calm demeanor of quarterback Johnny Unitas, who showed the kind of control with the football that people just loved. Late in the game, on a key play, a New York pass rush forced Unitas out of the pocket, and he calmly waved one of his receivers to move to another spot while the play was in motion before making his pass. Those kinds of images stick with people.

An ESPN.com article by Bob Carter talked about how much Unitas gave the Colts and what he meant as a leader. In that piece, Unitas' long-time favorite receiver, Raymond Berry, said that it "was his uncanny instinct for calling the right play at the right time, his icy composure under fire, his fierce competitiveness, and his utter disregard for his own safety" that led to so much success as the Baltimore quarterback.

Unitas' cool play made him a national star after that game, one that grew the following year when the Colts won the NFL title again thanks to a fourth-quarter comeback and a 31–16 victory over those same Giants, this time in Baltimore. The legend of the Colts and their love affair with the city was born.

Tom Matte was a running back in the 1960s and early '70s who helped the Colts to plenty of success during that time. In a previous book done with one of the authors, Matte spoke about the kind of relationship that the Colts had with their fans.

"I don't think there will ever be a sports team again that had the relationship the Colt players had with the fans," Matte said. "We live in a different time. There's free agency. There's no stability as far as your team goes. There's a lot of changeover. Maybe three or four guys would come into your team one year—max, maybe two—when I played with the Colts. You take a look at the wholesale changes that happened [in 2001] after they won the Super Bowl and they had to get the salary cap down."

Matte loved to talk about the special bond that still existed between fans and the former Colts, decades after the games stopped and the team had taken off for the Midwest. That bond reminds some people of the connections between fans and teams like the Packers, since it truly joined a city and fans. But many from outside the area recognized what existed in Baltimore during the glory days of the Colts.

It's starting to get to that point with the Ravens, something Matte noticed more than 10 years ago while working as a radio broadcaster for the team. And it reminded him of something that he'd seen before.

"They just love the Ravens, and it's a good thing," he said. "If you take a look at the Colts as they grew, all the people grew with the Colts and it became an older crowd. They lived and died with us. I mean, they knew our children's names, they knew our birthdays, we got birthday cards from fans. They'd write notes to you. We were such a part of the community."

They grew into the fabric of the community, a big reason that football became so ingrained in Baltimore, especially during the '60s. Charm City had, arguably, the best quarterback in the National Football League if not the most well-known, and even though the Colts went 11 seasons without winning another championship, they were feared. In fact, a sportswriter coined an unusual term to describe Memorial Stadium, calling it "The World's Largest Outdoor Insane Asylum."

That probably wasn't too much of an overstatement. The building proved very loud, and opposing teams did not love playing there. What made things even crazier is that good football was being played on a regular basis. The Baltimore Colts remained in the hunt for postseason play every year in the '60s. But the playoffs were much different in the NFL of those days. There weren't 12 teams making the playoffs like in today's world. In addition, free agency hadn't yet taken shape like today, a big reason if a team became good, it could easily stay that way for many years. Teams didn't have the annual worry about which players could leave when contracts expired.

The Colts made it back to the NFL championship in 1964, suffering a surprising 27–0 loss to the Cleveland Browns—the last time that team has won an NFL title. Baltimore then lost in a tiebreaker for a conference playoff game the following year despite losing its top two quarterbacks in the weeks leading up to the game. The Colts remained close in 1966 and just missed the playoffs in 1967 despite finishing with an 11–1–2 record and not losing a game until the season's final week. Thanks to the lack of wild cards, the Colts sat home while the Los Angeles Rams, holding the same 11–1–2 record, went to the playoffs and got blasted by eventual Super Bowl II champion Green Bay in the opening round.

The Colts made it to the Super Bowl the following season after going 13–1 in the regular season. But the New York Jets handed them a stunning 16–7 loss, a victory that Baltimore sports fans still grumble about today. That game probably had something to do with coach Don Shula leaving the team after a so-so 1969 season where they finished 8–5–1.

The NFL-AFL merger took place in 1970, and the Colts, Steelers, and Browns moved in with the American Football League teams to form the American Football Conference. Baltimore won the Super Bowl that season, and made it back to the AFC title game the year after. Then everything began to fall apart when Robert Irsay bought the team in the summer of 1972. Irsay immediately began attracting attention and controversy for his interesting behavior, and the Colts did something they hadn't done much of in the past—lose, and with regularity.

Baltimore had three good years during the mid-1970s, winning the AFC East from 1975 to 1977 before the wheels came off the cart. Irsay then began complaining about wanting a new stadium, flirting with other cities, and talking about new deals in different locations. But fans believed there was no way he would move the Colts. That just couldn't happen. The Colts were one of the best-supported franchises in the National Football League for years, a rock, a pillar of the community.

However, those attendance numbers slowly began dwindling as the losses piled up. The fans laughed at Irsay more, staying away in droves in the late '70s and early '80s, and the owner stepped up his search for a new address to house the Colts. Everything really kicked into high gear—apparently—after the 1983 season, one where a young Colts team truly appeared to be finding its way, thanks to a solid mix of younger players and veterans, guided by tough coach Frank Kush.

The offseason became a theatre of the absurd. The *Baltimore Sun*, in Irsay's obituary years later, talked about how he shopped the team around to cities like Phoenix, Memphis, Los Angeles, New York, Jacksonville, and Indianapolis. On January 20, 1984, reporters found Irsay at the Baltimore-Washington International Airport with then-Mayor William Donald Schaefer, and, according to the *Sun*'s story, barked at the media the following remark that will live on in Baltimore football infamy: "I have [no] intentions of moving the goddamn team," he yelled. "If I did, I would tell you about it, but I'm staying here."

The *Sun* also said in the obituary that "news leaks had prompted him to cancel a meeting that day with officials from Phoenix, where he was thinking of moving the team, and fly to Baltimore."

Two months later, the team was gone, spirited out of town on a cold and snowy March night with no notice, en route to Indianapolis. While no one was hurt or injured, and this subject remained only about sports, it became a night that Baltimoreans never forgot.

The move left Baltimore without a football team until Art Modell moved the Browns to Charm City for the 1996 season. Modell's move of that team stunned Cleveland in much the same manner, and it's the likely reason he's never made the Hall of Fame despite numerous contributions to the NFL on and off the field.

But the Baltimore fans never forgot that the Colts left—and the way they snuck out of town in the dark on a snowy night.

Years later, when the Colts came in from Indianapolis to play the Baltimore Ravens, Jim Irsay—Bob's son, who had taken over as the owner of the Midwest team—sat in the second row of the press box for that game. A number of Baltimore fans saw him. It didn't take them long to unleash a string of venomous hate, flipping him off, cursing him out, screaming, yelling. And this went on for the entire game. But to Irsay's credit, he never blinked or responded. The press box is a glass-enclosed structure in Baltimore, and the Indy owner had protection. Still, he didn't respond during those long three hours.

The Ravens took a little time to connect once they came to town. The situation might have been different if they were an expansion team, but some wondered if Baltimore had pulled the same stunt as Indianapolis. However, these kinds of moves were happening on a regular basis now, and Modell needed to make the move—any move—for financial reasons, pure and simple. The Ravens drew big crowds right away, starting in 1996, but it seemed to take a bit of time until the city connected. The first coach was Ted Marchibroda, who guided the old Colts during some of their better seasons in 1970s. He did a good job of helping a young team grow, but when Brian Billick took over in 1999, the Ravens seemed ready to take off. After three losing seasons under Marchibroda, the Ravens went 8–8 in Billick's first year before everything changed in 2000.

The offense struggled in the early days of that season, going five games without a touchdown but still posting a 5–4 mark after nine games. Billick made the move from Tony Banks to Trent Dilfer at quarterback and, after losing the first game with Dilfer in the job, they won all the rest and went on to a shocking Super Bowl triumph. That sealed the love affair between the city of Baltimore and the Ravens—a romance that would stay warm and fuzzy for a very long time.

STAN'S SIDEBAR

ON BALTIMORE'S RELATIONSHIP WITH THE RAVENS

I think the fact that Baltimore didn't have a team and were starved for a team really helped the Ravens. I know its influence; I'm a high school football coach, and high school football has gotten so much better since the Ravens have come because there's more interest in football now among all the kids. My kids didn't have anybody to follow growing up. I had a daughter in college and another going to college when they came. I think everybody was starved for a team because we kept hearing we were going to get an expansion team.

The fact that there was a base of Colts fans left over, pro football fans left over, was huge. And I think the Ravens did a good job of trying to tap into that, bringing Johnny Unitas to all the early games, having him stand on the sideline, having Lenny Moore involved, having a lot of the old Colts involved when they left Memorial Stadium. All those different things, I think, helped ingrain them in the community. It jumpstarted it.

If you expanded into Jacksonville at that time, they had a USFL team, and college football, but they didn't have a pro interest there, and it's never caught on in Jacksonville. They have to cover seats up there. Baltimore wasn't like that, and I think Art Modell knew that when he came here—that it was a place a lot like Cleveland. It had a lot of blue-collar, working-class football fans.

I think the Ravens caught on right away, and I think it grew because there was some reluctance from some of the old Colts people. But once their kids got involved, the old fans got involved, and it became a family thing again, like it was with the Colts. It took a little bit of time but I think it took a lot less time than it could have because there was a base here.

CHAPTER 18
DENNIS PITTA

Dennis Pitta missed most of the 2013 and 2014 seasons plus all of 2015 after suffering a pair of serious hip injuries. He underwent surgery twice, and many people felt the tight end would never play football again. But Pitta returned in 2016 and led all NFL tight ends in catches to become a huge part of the Baltimore offense.

The Baltimore Ravens were thrilled after crushing the Miami Dolphins 38–6, a game where tight end Dennis Pitta helped with nine catches for 90 yards and two touchdowns. Afterward, he heard about it from his coach and teammates.

"I feel great for Dennis," said coach John Harbaugh. "He won't take as much heat from all of us now. We've been on him pretty hard, pretty much all year. For him to break out like that…it was good to see. He played really well."

Those two touchdowns proved to be the only ones Pitta scored all season long, but that didn't matter on this day. The fact that he scored a touchdown—actually, the fact that Pitta was playing and helping the Ravens once again—well, that was the real story.

Pitta dislocated and fractured his right hip in training camp during the summer of 2013. He underwent surgery and made it back about four months later to play in the last four games in 2013, catching 20 passes for 169 yards and one touchdown. Naturally, his first game was played on a snowy, windy, and cold afternoon in Baltimore as the Ravens pulled out a wild 29–26 victory over Minnesota. Still, Pitta posted six catches and scored a touchdown in that game.

He made it through the rest of that season just fine, but he hurt that hip once more early in the following season against Cleveland. Pitta simply tried to turn and got hurt once more. His season had ended—after 16 catches in just three games—but a bigger question loomed large—would Pitta ever step on a football field again?

He did play again. But it took quite a while.

Pitta did not return to the field in 2014 and could not make it back the following year despite his attempts. He returned for the

213

start of the 2016 season, but no one was really sure what the tight end would—or could—do. In the season's first game, a 13–7 victory over Buffalo at home, Pitta made three catches for 39 yards and drew huge roars from the crowd every time.

"It was great just being out there," Pitta said that day. "Once you are back out there, it feels like you have been out there for the last couple of years."

Pitta said he loved having the chance to run through the well-known tunnel onto the field before the game and realizing that yes, he was back after two years.

"It was really cool," Pitta said. "Emotions ran high for me during that time. It was a special moment to run through the smoke and out of the tunnel in front of our fans again. It's been a while since I've been able to do that. I feel really good, and the legs feel good. I stayed healthy, which is important, and I am excited to keep it rolling."

He was fortunate enough to do just that throughout the rest of the 2016 season, once again growing into a big part of a Baltimore offense that struggled at times. Pitta finished the season with 86 catches for 729 yards, once more growing into one of Flacco's favorite targets in an offense that relied heavily on short passes.

And even though Pitta caught just two touchdown passes in 2016, he felt like he'd made a bigger point by being with the team all season long. The Ravens certainly needed him.

"Yes, I had a couple touchdowns today, but I feel like I have been producing all year," he said after the Miami game. "I don't think after a game like this, 'Oh, I'm back.' I feel like I've been back since Week 1. It feels good, though. I think that somebody mentioned that my last touchdown was 2013, and that was a long time ago."

Over a short period of time Pitta tried—in practice—to see if he would be ready to play in 2015 but the tight end wasn't quite there yet. The 2016 season proved to be a much different story, something that Flacco, who is one of Pitta's closest friends on the team, saw right after the first game.

"If he was coming back, I knew he would be productive," Flacco said. "Last year when he came back for a couple of weeks in practice, and they decided to not have him play, he looked good. He looked like himself. I think he's going to get more and more comfortable as the year goes on. We just have to keep him healthy."

They did that, and it paid off as Pitta's 86 catches quietly led all NFL tight ends. The Ravens are looking for more downfield threats from wide receivers to complement Pitta, something that would make their passing attack that much tougher to stop.

But there's no question the Ravens who played with him before the two surgeries were happy that Pitta was able to return in 2016 and contribute the way he did. The team certainly needed him.

"I don't know what he's been through," Flacco said. "He's the only person that really, really knows what he's been through. His wife, his parents—I'm sure they have a certain way they feel about it, but I just want him on the field. Listen, he's a special football player... He's been through a lot, and he's put a lot of work in.... He has been productive. I [feel] good for him."

The Ravens selected Pitta in the fourth round of the 2010 draft from Brigham Young. Tight end was a position the team had some concerns about since long-time starter Todd Heap would be starting his 10th—and what turned out to be final—season with the team.

But Pitta didn't produce much in that first season. The Ravens made the playoffs in coach John Harbaugh's third season as young quarterback Joe Flacco kept learning and developing. Heap made 40 catches for 599 yards and five touchdowns. Pitta, however, played in 10 games and made one catch for one yard in that first season.

Heap went to Arizona after that, and Pitta's production quickly increased. Ed Dickson led the tight ends with 54 catches that season. Pitta came on with 40 for 405 yards and three touchdowns. He really came on big in 2012, the year the Ravens made a late rush and surprised many by rolling to the Super Bowl title. That season saw Pitta finish with 61 catches for 669 yards and seven touchdowns, becoming one of Flacco's favorite targets for short and mid-range passes and taking over as the top tight end. Pitta also had four catches with a touchdown in the Super Bowl victory over the 49ers.

That's when everything began to fall down for Pitta. He got hurt in training camp the following summer, leaping up to make a catch and landing the wrong way. That set up surgery and rehab and, as noted, the tight end didn't make it back until the last part of the 2013 season.

Everything seemed to be fine in 2014 as he made 10 catches in a season-opening loss to the Bengals. He added three catches in the next two games, but the third game, in Cleveland, is where Pitta re-injured the hip, and all the old questions began to come up again.

In 2016, Pitta injured his finger during preseason, which cost the tight end some time, but he recovered from that and was ready when the regular season began.

Basically, all that meant was a little more work. He talked with the team's online reporter before the 2016 season about the fact that grinding away was what he needed to do.

"I've been around for a couple years and certainly don't think anything is going to be handed to me," Pitta said in that article. "We have a lot of tight ends in the building now, and I'm excited for that kind of competition. Hopefully I can earn a spot somewhere and add value to this team. That's really the thing that's important to me."

One thing that hurt the Ravens but helped Pitta was the preseason injury to newly acquired tight end Benjamin Watson. The veteran tore his Achilles tendon and was sidelined for the season, opening up some space for Pitta and others. Pitta stepped right in and became one of Flacco's top targets again.

Pitta caught four passes in the 2016 season-opening victory over Buffalo before going back to the spot of his 2014 injury—Cleveland. The tight end never looked better this time, catching nine passes for 102 yards as the Ravens rallied from a big early deficit and posted a 25–20 victory over the struggling Browns. It was a physical game, and Pitta even took a hit to that hip, but he walked away just fine.

"This is a great team win, and certainly one that's going to serve us down the road," Pitta said after the game.

When asked about how much it meant for him to turn in such a performance in the place where he got carted off the previous time, Pitta opened up a bit.

"Last time I was here, I didn't get to go home with everybody," Pitta said "Fortunately this time, I do. It's going to be a lot more fun this time around. I wasn't thinking about my hip going into this game, and rightfully so. I don't think it'd be doing myself [any good] to be thinking about it. I just feel fortunate to come out healthy. I'm feeling good."

He then talked about his whole situation with the hip injury and what he would be focusing on in the days going forward. Pitta turned out to be on the money with his statement as he got through the rest of the 2016 season without major incident and once again became one of the NFL's best tight ends.

"There's aches; there's pains," Pitta said. "That's just the grind of the season. I feel like I'm over the hump. There's no more hurdles for me to climb. It's not something I'm going to think about. I'm confident in how I feel, and how I'll feel going forward."

And he went forward just fine.

STAN'S SIDEBAR

ON DENNIS PITTA

Pitta got hurt the first time in training camp, and he came back at the end of that year. The second time, he got hurt in Cleveland. It was just a screen pass he took, and he went to cut, and the hip popped out again. Now, he had played the last third of the previous year on that injury without it affecting him. That's when he got the new contract. He came back and played well. The hip socket was dislocated and fractured—sort of like the Bo Jackson injury. They had to go back in and tighten that up so it didn't come out, and they didn't do a good enough job the first time. It came out again without being hit again, and you were thinking, *They'll never be able to fix this*. But he did all his research, found the right guy— Dr. Roger Wilber in Cleveland.

Pitta had confidence he could come back. A lot of people didn't think he could. But he felt he had a moral obligation to this team because they had paid him all that money when he wasn't playing. He came back to sort of repay that debt, and he lasted the whole year. People were always going "ooh" and "aah" when he got hit. But that, to me, wasn't the issue. It didn't pop out the second time on a collision. It popped out when he got into a bad angle. It just came out.

It's just like ACL injuries. Those are usually non-contact injuries. It just gives out when you hit the ground at the wrong angle. And that's even worse, because you never know when it can pop out. But Pitta was able to come out and catch 86, more than any tight end in the league in 2016, as far as catches are concerned. You've got to give him a lot of credit. I interviewed him after the last game of the season and told him I really respected him for coming back because of that reason, and he really risked his long-term health and mobility to pay off that debt. He took a big pay cut last year, and he earned much of it back. It was impressive to me because of the reason he did it. It wasn't because he wanted to make more money.

He had made a lot of money not playing, and he felt he owed it to his teammates and to the organization. But that's having a good organization. Not many people would feel that way about an organization. That means the players respect the organization to even feel that way. So I think that type of feeling is why the Ravens have been so successful.

CHAPTER 19
TERRELL SUGGS

One of the biggest comeback stories of the 2016 season for the Ravens was the return of linebacker Terrell Suggs. The man they call "Sizzle" suffered a torn Achilles tendon and played in just one game in 2015. Could he make it back now that he was older? Suggs had experienced the same injury in 2012 but returned to play eight games that season as the Ravens pulled off a stunning late-season run that led to the franchise's second Super Bowl triumph.

In 2016 Suggs played like he had throughout much of his career. He appeared in 15 games as the Ravens went 8–8, finishing with 33 tackles and eight sacks for a Baltimore defense that often played well but needed some help getting to the passer. Coach John Harbaugh talked about how well Suggs played that season after the Baltimore defense shut down Miami in a 38–6 rout that set up the team for a shot at the AFC North title—one that the Ravens didn't get.

"Very impressed with Terrell Suggs," Harbaugh said after the Miami game. "All of the things you mentioned speak volumes, but what speaks the loudest is just what you see on tape. He's doing it from the first play to the last play. Put the last three plays on when you get a chance, and just watch him play the last three plays on defense when the outcome of the game is very much in hand. Just watch how hard he played in those three plays. I think that tells the whole story."

Suggs has made a number of marks since coming to the Ravens as a first-round draft choice in 2003 out of Arizona State. The Ravens were trying to get back on their feet defensively after winning the Super Bowl in the 2000 season and losing to Pittsburgh in the AFC playoffs the following year. Baltimore already boasted a number of stars on defense like linebacker Ray Lewis and others, and Suggs eventually fit right in.

His bold, brash style meshed with Lewis and later with players like Ed Reed, Bart Scott, Bernard Pollard, and others. The Ravens told you a few things on defense—they were big, bad, bold, and tough, and they'd be coming after you. More often than not, offenses would have trouble against them, and the Ravens were just fine predicting that before it happened.

And Suggs took on an even bigger role after Reed, Lewis, Pollard, and others left over time. Many fans in other cities didn't love the Ravens, especially in the early days under Billick when they were so good defensively, because of their loud and brash ways.

Suggs, as mentioned, took right to that and kept on going the longer he played. He knew where the cameras were, knew what to say, knew how to draw a bit of attention to the Ravens. When Suggs essentially took over as the defensive leader, he did more of the same but in a softer way than Lewis, who would often be talking and yelling and screaming.

Suggs had a biting, sarcastic sense of humor that he knew how to use well. He's often poked fun at Tom Brady—and others. But Suggs seemed more careful at times about what he said. It was almost like he was watching it a bit. The Ravens, quite simply, haven't been as loud and brash and bold under Harbaugh—and that seemed to suit the coach just fine.

Through the 2016 season, Suggs was the team's all-time leader in sacks with 114.5, sack yards (822), and fumbles forced (32). He also topped the team in postseason sacks (12.5) and yards (79). Also, Suggs ranked second in tackles through 2016 (856) behind only Ray Lewis in the Baltimore record books.

But Suggs isn't the type of athlete who will stand up and quote stats to the media or on camera. Suggs isn't that way. He loves to use examples, different types of humor, and make people laugh. That's just his way, and he does it well.

Suggs displayed this after the Ravens scored a tough late-season victory over the Bengals in 2016. Baltimore had problems with Cincinnati at times in recent seasons—the Ravens would often lose to the Bengals in the final game of the season on the road—but Suggs made some good points about what it felt like to beat the team that had handled them in recent meetings.

"It feels good. Like I said, when you're fighting a kid in the schoolyard, and he's always beating you, and you finally punch him in the mouth, maybe he'll quit picking on you," Suggs said. "But like I said, we've got to see these guys again. They came out, and they came out to win. They played a tremendous game. We finally got over the little Bengal hump. They didn't have [A.J. Green]. I wish he was out there. I'd like for them to be full go [with] A.J. Green. But also, you've got to be careful what you wish for, so we'll take it, man. We'll take it."

Suggs truly grew into a leader as time went on, especially after Lewis retired following the 2012 season. For years, one of the trademarks of a Ravens' home game was for Lewis to do a dance coming out of the tunnel—always the team's last player to enter the field—when Baltimore would take the field before the game. Suggs now does his own thing going through the tunnel.

Lewis was the unquestioned leader of the defense when he joined the team in 1996. In fact, the timing helped Lewis as the team had just moved to Baltimore that year and was kind of looking for some people to take charge, and the rookie linebacker did.

Suggs joined the crowd on the aforementioned brash defense and took off when he was drafted in 2003.

In his first season, Suggs finished with 33 tackles and 12 sacks, a rookie franchise record, helping the Ravens get more pressure on quarterbacks throughout the season. Interestingly, Suggs started just one game that season. Yet he finished tied for seventh in the NFL in sacks and was named the NFL's Defensive Rookie of the Year.

The Ravens had picked him 10th overall in the previous spring's NFL draft. He likely caught the eye of the Baltimore scouts and coaches with his Division I-A record of 24 sacks the previous season at Arizona State. Suggs kept right on going in the NFL, even though he didn't play every down.

Baltimore may have gotten a break with Suggs thanks to one simple number. When he ran at some pre-draft workouts, his time in the 40-yard dash was slower than some teams might have liked. Therefore he slipped to the No. 10 spot in the draft.

"I wasn't concerned at all," Suggs said at a post-draft conference call. "I thought I was going to be judged [on how I] play football, not judged how I was going to do in track speed, but that's what happened, and it happened. I'm a football player, so I'm not really stressing about anything else."

He showed his skills early and often in that first season with a Baltimore defense that was still good but not quite at the level it had been a few years before when the Ravens won the Super Bowl. Suggs would help lead them back.

"He's a bright kid," then-Ravens defensive coordinator Mike Nolan said in an Associated Press article when the Defensive Rookie of the Year award was announced. "Terrell's still got a lot of growing up to do, but he learns quickly, has a tremendous passion for football and isn't intimidated by the pro game."

Suggs worked out of the team's 3–4 formation that season, often rushing out of the outside as a linebacker and doing well. He eventually grew into his role as a defensive leader and, although first known for his pass-rushing skills, Suggs could give the team more and was a player that other offenses feared.

Suggs' numbers and awards grew as time went on. He made the Pro Bowl six times—in 2004, 2006, 2008, 2010, 2011, and 2013. The last time came after he missed half of 2012 with the Achilles' injury. Suggs also was chosen as a first alternate in 2014 and a second alternate in 2016. Thirteen years after being drafted, Suggs still has plenty of sizzle left. That's not surprising at all for this guy.

CHAPTER 20
THE 2012 SUPER BOWL RUN

Coach John Harbaugh walked into the indoor practice area at the team's training facility on Wednesday, January 2, 2013, and seemed kind of grim. That didn't really catch anyone's attention, because coaches have periods when they act that way. They're upset about this or that and certainly don't want the media to see the source of their concern. Harbaugh answered about 20 questions, and one of them involved Ray Lewis, their veteran linebacker who'd been out since tearing his tricep in a win over Dallas in October.

The first question from the media involved the coach's thoughts about how hard Lewis was working to get back to the field, since some felt that 2012 could and/or would be the linebacker's final season. Harbaugh said he wouldn't commit to whether Lewis would return for the start of the playoffs that Sunday when the Colts were coming to town, but the coach admitted to being impressed with how hard the defensive leader worked to give it a shot. Harbaugh answered several more questions before the linebacker came out.

When Lewis greeted the media a few minutes later, he began dropping a few hints that the possibility of him playing certainly existed. "Let's just say I'm active on the roster," he said. "We'll see from there." Lewis then answered a few more questions, coming closer and closer to revealing his main point. And then, when asked about his longterm plans, the answer came—in almost cryptic fashion.

"Today, I told my team that this would be my last ride. And I told them I was just at so much peace in where I am with my decision because of everything that I've done in this league," Lewis said. "I've done it. I've done it, man. There's no accolade that I don't have individually...and now, God is calling. God is calling in so many areas of life. My children have made the ultimate sacrifice for their father. I've done what I wanted to do in this business and now it's my turn to give them back something. So, it's either hold on to the game and keep playing and let my kids miss out on times that we can be sharing together. One of the hardest things in the world is to walk away from my teammates, because that's my brotherhood. I think we all get to enjoy what Sunday will feel like knowing that this will be the last time 52 plays in a uniform in [the] Ravens stadium."

The announcement clearly affected his teammates, because Lewis had been with Baltimore since the team began play in town in 1996. He was the team's second first-round draft pick that season and had turned into a likely Hall of Famer. But on the field, with the team, he was a leader that they loved and followed.

That's the message that fellow linebacker Terrell Suggs talked about later that day.

"I'm not going to lie to you; it affected me because for the past 10 years of my career, I've been sitting right next to the man and going to war on Sundays with the man," Suggs said. "When he went up there [in the team meeting], I thought we were getting our 'let's go on a run [in] the playoffs' speech. Not that. Come Sunday, it will be the last time, potentially, he and I will be at [the stadium] together. It's going to be one hard last time; we need to make it one to remember."

They did just that, playing hard and beating the young Colts 24–9. The Lewis announcement clearly seemed to give the team an emotional lift. And maybe that was good for them at that time. The Ravens clearly were playing for Lewis now. They wanted to send him out with a championship. They wanted him to go out in style, which is just what happened as Baltimore stunned Denver and New England with road victories before edging the 49ers 34–31 in a wild Super Bowl in New Orleans.

"When Ray Lewis announced his retirement, we all came together," wide receiver/kick returner Jacoby Jones said during a Super Bowl week press conference. "We're going to make sure we send him out with a victory."

And that's just what they did.

There had been some questions about the Ravens before season's end. They started 9–2 and often looked good doing it, something that was even more impressive since injuries really hurt the team with players like Lewis, Haloti Ngata, and Suggs out for stretches.

But they stumbled to the finish line, losing four out of the final five yet still winning the AFC North Division with a 10–6 record. Were they going to be able to get it back together again for the playoffs? Could the Ravens start playing like they did in the first 11 games—and not the last five?

The answer was yes. After beating the Colts in what turned out to be Lewis' final home game, the Ravens went to Denver, a team that had whipped them in Baltimore 34–17 in December. However, the Ravens turned things around in Colorado, pulling off a stunning 38–35 victory in double overtime that advanced them to the AFC Championship game against old playoff rival New England.

The Ravens forced the Denver game into overtime thanks to one of the most dramatic plays in team history. Trailing 35–28, the Ravens were stuck at their own 30-yard line in the final moments of the fourth quarter, facing third-and-3 and seeming all but out of it. Denver's defense then let Jones somehow slide behind their deep coverage on the right side, and Flacco threw a deep pass through the cold, thin Denver air that the receiver caught. He then went into the end zone for a stunning touchdown with 31 seconds left. Justin Tucker added the extra point, and the game was headed for overtime.

Tight end Dennis Pitta said a few days later that he wasn't surprised that Flacco had a big game against Denver.

"In these critical games in the playoffs, we know he's going to come up huge for us," Pitta said.

Tucker later added the game-winning field goal from 47 yards out early in the second overtime. That gave the Ravens one of the most shocking wins in their history. People then started to wonder—was this their year? Could they do it for Lewis? Flacco sure tried to help. He completed 18-of-34 passes for 331 yards and three touchdowns without an interception.

They'd need more of the same against the Patriots in the AFC title game, a team they could have beaten the year before if not for some late miscues—a dropped pass from Lee Evans in the end zone, which would have given them the win, followed by a badly missed field goal from Billy Cundiff that would have tied the game and forced overtime. Instead, they suffered a brutal loss as the Pats went on to the Super Bowl.

The Ravens, though, were getting that chance once again, just one year later, and Harbaugh was thrilled the week of the game to be given that opportunity.

"It would be hard to imagine, for me, a more exciting thing that being in the NFL playoffs and getting to [the AFC] championship game and ultimately the Super Bowl," he said that week. "That's what it's all about. To me, it's the pinnacle of the sport."

The Ravens struggled in the first part of this New England game, trailing 13–7 at halftime as the offense didn't do a great job of moving the ball until the second quarter wore on. But the second half was a different story as the Ravens scored all 21 points en route to a 28–13 victory.

Baltimore took the lead when Flacco hit Pitta with a five-yard touchdown pass in the third quarter. Flacco then made it 21–13 when he threw a three-yard touchdown pass to Anquan Boldin on the first play of the fourth quarter. The Patriots fumbled on their next drive, and the Ravens recovered at the Patriots 47-yard line. Flacco later threw an 11-yard touchdown pass to Boldin for a 28–13 lead with 11:13 left. Once again, Flacco threw for three touchdowns without an interception.

After that, the Ravens stopped the Pats on downs and twice picked off quarterback Tom Brady to seal the victory and stamp their ticket to the Super Bowl. Now the Super Bowl always features plenty of atmosphere and flash and side stories, but this one had something very unusual—two brothers coaching against each other as John Harbaugh would be facing Jim Harbaugh, the coach of the San Francisco 49ers.

John Harbaugh said the day after the New England game that it would be a great time for his whole family, and he wasn't worrying about battling his brother just yet

"I can't wait to see them down there in New Orleans," he said at a press conference. "It's going to be a great time."

The Ravens—led by Flacco and Jones—experienced the most fun in the first part of the game. Flacco threw three touchdown passes in the first half as the Ravens rolled to a 21–6 halftime lead, seemingly doing whatever they wanted on offense as the 49ers couldn't accomplish nearly as much.

Jacoby Jones, who just kept making big plays at the right time during the season, and especially in the playoffs, came through yet again. He caught a 56-yard touchdown pass from Flacco late in the first half. That turned out to be a wild play where Jones snagged the pass while falling but had the presence of mind to jump to his feet. Since no San Francisco defender had touched him, he faked out two players before running into the end zone for the touchdown. After that, Jones brought back the second-half kickoff for a 108-yard touchdown and a 22-point lead.

That's when things went a bit wacky. Moments later, the lights in one part of the building went out as the building went through a 34-minute power outage. (Some reports said it was 35 minutes.) For some reason, though, the power problems seemed to help San Francisco, which came back from the delay playing much better football than before.

"Obviously, the [break] didn't go well for us," Baltimore offensive lineman Marshal Yanda later told *Sports Illustrated*. "We were sluggish getting back in sync. The 49ers had all the momentum. We were reeling."

The 49ers cut the lead to 31–29 and had a chance to tie the game with 9:57 left, but quarterback Colin Kaepernick's pass to Randy Moss on the two-point conversion was far off, letting the Ravens hang on to the lead. The Ravens added a field goal to make it 34-29 with 4:19 left.

San Francisco marched back downfield again. The 49ers got to first-and-goal deep in Baltimore territory, but the Ravens held on as cornerback Jimmy Smith made two big plays at the end. The Ravens blitzed hard in that final series, trying to make Kaepernick beat them with throws, and he wasn't able to do it. On fourth-and-goal from the 5-yard line, Smith played tight defense as the 49ers quarterback rolled right and tried to throw it to Michael Crabtree. But Baltimore put on a blitz, and Kaepernick threw it too high and far.

Coach Jim Harbaugh screamed for pass interference but no flag was thrown. The Ravens then ran the ball three times but did not want to punt. Instead, punter Sam Koch ran around in the back of the end zone until four seconds remained, getting out of bounds for a safety that made it 34–31. The ensuing free kick went to Ted Ginn Jr., but Baltimore's Josh Bynes tackled him after a 31-yard return and the Ravens had their second Super Bowl win.

"I think it is fitting that we won that way," Flacco said when speaking to the media that day. "We are a tough, blue-collar city, and that's the way our games kind of come down. We were up 28–6, and I'm sure a lot of people were nervous but were kind of like, 'This one might be pretty easy.' And the next thing you know, the Niners get right back into it and play great football, and we had to grind it out."

Flacco finished by completing 22-of-33 for 287 yards for three touchdowns. Overall in the postseason, Flacco posted stellar statistics. He completed 73-of-126 for 1,140 yards with 11 touchdowns and no interceptions at all. That proved crucial in games where the Ravens were on the road and needed to come back a few times.

The combination of Flacco's strong play and the team wanting to win for Lewis as he finished his career proved enough. A quote from Suggs that the Ravens posted on their site showed how the team felt about Lewis:

"Ultimate cake," Suggs said. "There will never be another leader like him, and we sent him out like his brothers, and his legacy will go untainted."

STAN'S SIDEBAR

ON THE CHAMPIONSHIP

Well, in the regular season they lost four of their last five games. But the fifth game against Cincinnati, they had clinched the division, and they didn't play anybody. Plus, they got Haloti Ngata back, they got Ed Reed back, they got Ray Lewis back, and he announced his retirement. They had just reshuffled the offensive line around.

I still have a text that I sent to John the night they clinched the division. They lost the next-to-last game of the season but because, I think, Pittsburgh lost that night too, everybody was saying the Ravens backed into it. I sent him a text saying, "No, you never back into it. It's very hard to make the playoffs. I only did it like three years out of the 11 years I was in the NFL, and you're going to get everybody back, and you've got a really good chance to make a run in these playoffs." And he texted right back, saying something like, "You lifted my soul," or something like that.

Baltimore came in and went through the playoffs, and they just had a great run. They started off with the Colts and beat the Colts pretty badly here. Then they went out to Denver.

Everybody in Denver was planning for the next week with New England coming there. They thought it was a foregone conclusion they were going to win this game. But I was down on the field when Jacoby Jones caught that last-second pass. I was standing maybe 25 yards from Joe Flacco. He ran up like he was throwing a javelin and threw that ball. I couldn't see it. I just heard radio play-by-play announcer Gerry Sandusky saying in my ear, "He caught it and he's going for a touchdown." It was just crazy. It was like zero degrees down there. All of a sudden, it was warm, and everybody's running around, and Tucker kicks the winning field goal in overtime, and I remember running out and interviewing him on the field afterward. It was just one of those days where it was almost like divine intervention. I felt like there was a purpose there.

Then they go to New England. The year before, everybody on the Baltimore sideline thought they had won. Then they thought they were going to tie it, and then they lost. I remember going into the locker room after that game, and I wasn't going to interview kicker Billy Cundiff, who missed the game-tying kick that would have sent the game into overtime. I just went up to him. He just came up and put his arms around me and hugged me. He needed somebody to hug, I think, because he felt so bad at that point, and I had a decent relationship with him. I just knew he felt so bad. I just wanted to go up and put my hand on his shoulder, and he just put his arms around me and hugged me. I just felt so bad for him at that point.

And then, to think about that locker room the next year, where they went in there after the win over the Patriots, and CBS and Jim Nantz is in the locker room, and then they stop and show their faith with a big prayer in front of the whole country in winning that game. To come back and do what they did compared to the year before. Just a vast difference in those two locker rooms. It was so unbelievable. The joy was heightened because of what happened the year before. I know every guy who was there the year before remembered what it felt like in that locker room, and to go back in there and win that game was great.

What I remember about that game was the whole crowd behind the bench—all the New England fans had left, and all the Ravens fans had migrated over behind the bench, and you looked up and they were just going crazy. Security was telling Gerry Sandusky and those guys, "Get these people out of here." Like he could do something! He was in our booth. He was waving his arms, and they're telling him don't incite the fans.

I was on the field right where that ball was dropped the year before, and then to be on the field the next year at the end, and to turn around and see it, it looked like we were home. All the Ravens fans had filled the seats where the New England people had left. It was an unbelievable picture.

Then they had the Super Bowl. Harbaugh vs. Harbaugh. I think it actually motivated them. Was it a distraction? I'm sure it was a little bit of a distraction, having to answer that question over and over again. They did the best they could. John tried to downplay that. What can you really say differently? But I'm sure he had to look over on the sideline at times to see how or what his brother was doing or how he was reacting to things. It's just natural. If it was my brother, I'm sure I would have been looking over there to see. I'm sure he looked over there and saw Jim going crazy after that play, calling for holding and all that stuff.

I remember I interviewed Jack Harbaugh after the game, walking off the field. His mixed emotions—so happy for John, but so sad for Jim. I think you have to choose to go the happy route at that point and then deal with the sad route later on, because you don't want to rain on one of your son's parades. Both of those guys are just disciples of their father. I think that last play really needed to be a no-call at that point, especially with the ball being thrown so poorly.

And that was another thing. John Harbaugh went up when they got to the 5-yard line, and he said, "Okay, we're going all-out blitz every play down here." He said that to Dean Pees. "We're going to go after them." Because quarterback Colin Kaepernick could have easily run. He's such a running threat. John's thought was, "We're not to going to let them run the ball in. We're going to make Kaepernick make the perfect throw to beat us," and he couldn't do it. It was a great move. At that point, forget the game plan; this is what we're doing. You've got to go with your gut at that point, and John's gut was right. It was first-and-7 from the 7-yard line, and they went four plays and got nothing. The Ravens went all-out blitz, and they got right in the grill of Kaepernick. He had to just throw it to an area, and he miscalculated the area.

Jacoby Jones was fast, number one. I remember going into that Denver locker room after that playoff game. He took off his pads and the shirt he had on underneath said FAST AS HELL, and he showed it in that game. He had that great speed, and the Ravens knew how to take advantage of it, and he had good eyes on the returns. He had the uncanny ability to see at levels. If I cut here, I can cut there and go. It's not just one cut; it's one cut with the anticipation of the second cut on special teams. So he was able to make big plays on special teams, and he became that third receiver who just forced defenses. With him and Torrey Smith, it was just, "Who's the deep guy? Which one do we concentrate on?"

Jones is just one of the funniest guys. You know the great horse Secretariat, right? So he said to John, "You know Coach, I'm just like that horse Sagittarius." He also went on a show with Sandusky, and one of the things coaches always say is that teams end up losing a game more often than winning a game. The other team makes mistake to lose. Jacoby said more teams lose every week than win every week, and Gerry said it's half and half. And Jacoby said, "No, my coach told me more teams lose than win," and he couldn't be convinced otherwise because John told him that.

At the Denver game, I thought they were dead when Jacoby dropped the ball on fourth down on the previous series. They were down there, then they forced three-and-out, and Denver ran the ball. Denver did what they should have done: took time off the clock. So the Ravens got the ball back, they hit one or two short passes, and then Joe Flacco scrambled around. I remember I was right on the yard line where Joe was—and it looked like he threw a javelin. You know how you run up, you reach way back, and throw it? That's exactly what he did. I couldn't see the other end, but I had Gerry in my ear, and I heard he got it, and I looked down and the bench was going crazy.

After that fourth-down play, it looked like it was over. It looked like they might not even get the ball back. But they did and came up with that play. At that point, you just felt like God was in control and that this was going to happen. I only bring that up about God because about a month before the end of the season, I was on the state board of the Fellowship of Christian Athletes, and I asked John Harbaugh to speak at our banquet. He said, "Yeah, I'll do that." I'm not big on saying God talks to me. It's only happened maybe twice in my life. But I kept hearing something special was going to happen out of this. When that happened, I just said, "I can't believe it. God, did that happen?" And I shared that with John in the locker room. I still have the texts that we sent back and forth at that time, because he has a pretty strong faith, too.

So, that happened in the locker room, and the next week they went to New England where the year before there had been such disappointment, and they beat them there and then the Super Bowl. It was just unbelievable, all of the things that happened. Nobody beats New England up there in the playoffs. And when we were in Denver, they were already planning for New England to come there the next week. They thought this was a formality—to beat the Ravens. I'm sure the players took it seriously. But the fans didn't take it seriously at all. They thought there was no chance they were going to lose that game. That was Manning's first year out there. But he was Peyton Manning, and he had taken them all that way, and it was just unbelievable for the Ravens to win that game and then go up to New England and win that game. It was an unbelievable run. It was like a fairytale. Remember, Baltimore lost four out of their last five games.

Everybody said they shouldn't even be in the playoffs. But I was very optimistic, even though they lost some players at season's end, because of all those players who were coming back.

CHAPTER 21

JAMAL LEWIS

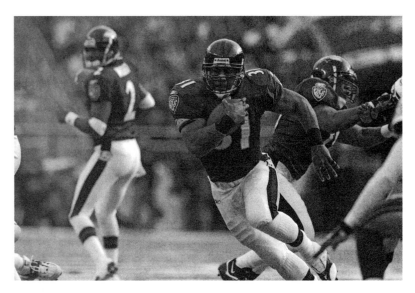

Running back Jamal Lewis gave the Ravens a rare mix of power and speed. He could run over, around, and through most defenders. He ran for a then-NFL record 295 yards versus Cleveland in 2003 and compiled 2,066 yards that season. Lewis was picked as the NFL's Offensive Player of the Year, carrying a Baltimore offense that experienced major passing issues.

Jamal Lewis provided the Baltimore Ravens with an unusual combination when they picked him in the first round of the 2000 draft out of Tennessee. He was picked fifth overall, as the Ravens were looking for a tough running back who could help carry their offense. But Lewis, well, he was kind of different.

He came into the NFL at 5'11", 245 pounds—after suffering a serious knee injury at college—and could beat you two ways. Lewis could run right over a player or race past them with ease. It's why he became one of the greatest runners of his time and so very hard to stop. Teams often couldn't figure out the right way to corral him, a task made even tougher by the fact that he ran behind a huge offensive line led by future Hall of Famer Jonathan Ogden at left tackle.

Running backs with big-time speed usually didn't weigh around 240. They often came thinner and taller than 5'11". Not this time. When at this best, Lewis had no problems speeding away from people or simply crushing them. That helped the Ravens offense because they often had problems at the quarterback position during those years thanks to struggling players like Kyle Boller, Chris Redman, and others.

Lewis showed many of his talents in the second game of the 2003 season when the Ravens played the Cleveland Browns at home. Baltimore wore white jerseys instead of purple at home that day, and the offense was ready to do some other unusual things after falling to Pittsburgh in the season opener the week before. Actually, what happened versus Cleveland began with the problems in the previous week's 34–15 drubbing in the Steel City.

According to *Sports Illustrated* and many other publications, Lewis told a few Browns during the week that if the Ravens let him carry the ball 30 times, he'd have "a career game." The Ravens gave the ball to Lewis just 15 times in the Pittsburgh game, and with rookie quarterback Kyle Boller clearly looking to find his way, running more could help.

"I want to take the pressure off [Boller]," Lewis said in the *Sports Illustrated* article.

That's exactly what happened on a sunny afternoon in Baltimore. Lewis set an NFL record with 295 yards on his 30 carries in a 33–13 rout. (Adrian Peterson now holds the record at 296.)

"Just a great day," Lewis said years later when talking with the team's website reporter. "I knew I could have a good day, but you don't think about setting records. Our plan was to pound them that day. I did want to get the single-game rushing record after seeing Corey Dillon [Cincinnati] run for so much my rookie year. That day's a great memory for me and my family. One of the greatest days of my life, having success doing something I loved."

Lewis posted 118 yards in the first quarter and 180 in the first half. There would have been more if not for a holding penalty during a 60-yard sprint in that opening half. The Browns held him to 15 yards in the third quarter, but Lewis then answered with 100 more yards in the final period, which included a 63-yard touchdown run at the start of the quarter.

On his first carry, 59 seconds into the game, Lewis burst free up the middle for an 82-yard touchdown run. His second carry was a 23-yard gain. Two carries, 105 yards—a good way to start any game.

But there was more still ahead. The Ravens ran well against Cleveland during those years, and they kept going with Lewis and his big offensive line leading the way, sparked by players like Jonathan Ogden, Edwin Mulitalo, Mike Flynn, and others. Today's pass-happy NFL might not see as many performances like this, but with a rookie quarterback at the helm, the Ravens knew they could lean on Lewis and run a lot—and so they did that day, letting him nearly break the 300-yard barrier.

Overall, the 2003 season turned out to be a dream for Lewis and a nightmare for Baltimore's opponents. He led the NFL with 2,006 yards, the third-best in NFL history. Stats like that helped him be named the NFL Offensive Player of the Year.

"[It was an] unbelievable year," Lewis said on the team's website years later. "Our quarterback [Kyle Boller] got hurt, and we ran the ball. Our line was great. They made the holes for me. I felt what we accomplished—with all my rushing yards—was good for the city of Baltimore. Good for all of us. Kind of a proud moment, a pick-me-up for the city."

Lewis said that year he was just glad to be able to help the Ravens on offense.

"I don't count how many carries I get, and I don't keep track of the yards," Lewis said back then. "I know how many yards I have because someone in the media is always telling me. I just put one foot in front of the other and let the yards add up, hopefully to help win games."

The Ravens won the AFC North with a 10–6 record that year but stumbled in the playoffs, losing a home game in the first round when Tennessee handed them a 20–17 defeat on a field goal in the final minute.

The Titans, determined not to let the Ravens beat them with Lewis and their ground game, knew Baltimore wasn't strong at throwing the ball—the Ravens were ranked last in the NFL there—and put up to nine men on the line, making running lanes tough to find and forcing Baltimore to pass. The Titans held Lewis to 35 yards on only 14 carries.

"They committed their resources to stop the run, and they did a great job," Billick said the next day. "I mean, they were set to stop the ball, and we made some plays outside—obviously not enough. [Lewis] ran for over 2,000 yards. I think we handed the ball off enough to him."

In 2007, Lewis moved on to the Browns, where he played until 2009, eventually stopping during that season when, according to the Cleveland *Plain Dealer*, "[his] season was shut down…by team doctors after examining the results of an MRI that showed abnormalities probably caused by excessive trauma to his brain." Lewis had already said 2009 would be the final year for him any way.

But most fans will remember him as a Raven and for the successes he experienced in Baltimore. The franchise's season ticket holders picked Lewis as one of the team's 10 best players during their first 20 years. He played with the team from 2000 to 2006, although he didn't play at all during 2001 when he suffered a season-ending knee injury in training camp.

Lewis ran for 7,801 yards during his six seasons with the Ravens and earned a spot in the team's Ring of Honor. He started with a bang, stepping into a starting role in 2000 and playing a big role in helping a struggling offense get just enough production to help an amazing defense push the team to the Super Bowl title.

In that first season, coach Brian Billick was once again trying to figure out who his quarterback would be, but the Ravens sure had a running back. Even though Billick came from a Minnesota offense that loved to throw, he couldn't quite do that yet in Baltimore—in fact, that strategy never came to fruition during his time with the team. So he would often turn to Lewis, something that began during his rookie year.

Trent Dilfer took over as quarterback midway through the season, but Lewis remained consistent. He finished the season with 1,364 yards and six touchdowns. The Ravens won their final seven games that year to finish at 12–4 and make the playoffs as the No. 4 seed. They beat Denver at home, shocked Tennessee and Oakland, and earned a trip to the Super Bowl.

The Ravens needed Lewis' help, because even though Dilfer played well at times, he also struggled. A consistent running game carried Baltimore that season, and the same formula worked in the playoffs. Dilfer made a few big plays here and there, but the team's phenomenal defense usually led the way—with some help from Lewis and the ground game.

Lewis ran for 338 yards and four touchdowns in four playoff games. He capped it off with a 102-yard, two-touchdown effort in the 34–7 whipping of the New York Giants in the Super Bowl. That ended his rookie year in style but turned out to be the last time Lewis would ever play in a winning playoff game.

He also dealt with some other issues away from football, serving a two-game suspension in 2004 for violating the NFL's substance abuse policy and then going to jail for four months (plus two more in a halfway house) after a plea bargain following federal drug charges.

After his career, Lewis, like many pro athletes, ran into financial difficulties. The Ravens gave him a ring after winning Super Bowl XLVII at the end of the 2012 season. But the *Baltimore*

Sun reported that it was put up for auction and later sold, and the Ravens said they were aware of the situation.

"Jamal Lewis informed us that he was forced to sell the Super Bowl XLVII ring due to financial difficulties," the team said in a statement. "We understand and respect his decision."

STAN'S SIDEBAR

ON JAMAL LEWIS

I remember we interviewed Brian Billick the night before the draft. They had the fifth pick, I think, and we asked, "Would you take a running back who's injured?" Because they needed a running back. He said, "I wouldn't leave that out of the equation." I didn't think they would. You know, it's too much of a gamble to take a guy that high who's coming off of knee surgery. But their doctors did a great job in finding out that Jamal Lewis could be healthy again and play at that level, and the next day they drafted him.

It was a surprise; everybody thought it was a reach. That's why they made it to the Super Bowl, because they could run the football, and Lewis became one of the great running backs of his era, no doubt about it. He had speed and size, the ability to break tackles, the ability to see the hole, and once he got through, he turned a five-yard run into a 40-yard run, and that's what great backs do. They break that one tackle. You have to be able to make somebody miss or run over somebody to be a great back in this league.

You're never going to be completely blocked where you don't get touched. He could do that with his speed, and he could do that with his power. The 2,000-yard year he had is one of the great years in the history of all running backs. I think the greatest year is O.J. Simpson when he first did it, because he did it in 14 games, and nobody had ever done it before. O.J. had a lot of long runs because of his speed.

Jamal carried the ball a lot of times and took a big pounding and still came back for more every game. He didn't miss time. He was there every game. His size and his speed are a rare combination that you don't see very often. I played against a few guys, like Herschel Walker, who had the big size and the speed, but you don't see it very often in any running back.

CHAPTER 22

THE LEAGUE'S MOST FEARSOME DEFENSE

When the Ravens came to town in 1996, they initially weren't known for their defense. In that first year, as the team adjusted to Baltimore and the city figured out what it was like to have a pro football team once more, defense did not become their calling card.

The numbers showed that. Baltimore allowed 441 points in a 4–12 season. That's nearly 28 points per game, and they ended up as the third-worst in the NFL that year. Baltimore had Ray Lewis, the rookie linebacker who flew all over the field making plays, but not much else at first.

Slowly, though, things began to change. The Ravens chose linebackers Peter Boulware and Jamie Sharper in the next season's draft plus defensive back Kim Herring. They also signed strong defensive lineman Michael McCrary as an unrestricted free agent before the 1997 season to give the team a much-improved pass rush. The next year, they added defensive back Duane Starks, who grew into a starter. In 1999, they brought in cornerback Chris McAlister, who also became a starter.

Then in 2000, they drafted Adalius Thomas, and he later grew into a multi-talented weapon who moved all over the field. The Ravens also made other free-agent moves and deals. They already had Rob Burnett on the defensive line but eventually brought in Tony Siragusa and Sam Adams. They also added Rod Woodson in the secondary plus a number of solid role players that gave the defense speed, talent, and depth that few could deal with.

So within four years, defense became the Baltimore Ravens' hallmark. They dominated teams during the 2000 season, as the Ravens gave up just 165 points in 16 games. They allowed just one touchdown through four playoff games, wrapping it up with a

Michael McCrary was one of the team's best free-agent signings. McCrary gave the Ravens a solid pass rush that it lacked in the late 1990s. He helped the team build a fearsome defense, something that paid off with a dominant performance throughout the 2000 season as Baltimore rolled to a Super Bowl title.

34–7 victory over the Giants in Super Bowl XXXV. New York's only score came on a kickoff return.

The argument has gone on for many years about whether that team had the best defense of all time. Lewis earned Super Bowl MVP honors, and the New York *Daily News* reported after the game that the linebacker said as much.

"This win is something they can't take away from us," Lewis said. "We are the best ever, the best ever right now. We didn't just break records, we shattered them. We dominated, literally."

Lewis actually drew the most attention due to his off-the-field issues the year before. But Billick knew how to take the pressure off Lewis—at least some of it—during the first part of Super Bowl week when the coach met with the media. It was a bold move, but it worked, as many media people were talking about Billick and what he said, instead of Lewis' well-known problems from 12 months before.

"Before you ask any questions, I know the Giants will have a curfew," Billick said. "We will not. I know you are going to ask Ray and me a lot of questions. He answered all of those questions last June. Just because someone wants to ask about it again doesn't mean Ray or I, or any of the Ravens, have to address it again."

After that, the Ravens became known for their defense—all the time. If anyone talked about Baltimore, defense would be the first subject. And defense proved to be what helped the team through periods when the offense had problems. The Ravens never really had a solid starting quarterback until they drafted Joe Flacco in 2008, and Baltimore needed the defense as a backbone. The offense wasn't going to score 30 points every game, but the defense made sure they wouldn't give up that many points.

That remains a bit of a mantra with the team; people look at the defense first, because that's what the Ravens have been known for. Even though the defense stumbled toward the end of the 2016 season, it helped carry the team and kept them in the playoff hunt throughout the year. Teams found it nearly impossible to run against the Ravens at times, and defensive tackle Brandon Williams talked about that following a late-season 38–6 rout of the Miami Dolphins.

"We're the number one run defense in the league right now; that's what we do," he said. "We execute, stay together as a group, and we get the job done. That's how our defense is—it's all 11 to the football. If someone misses a tackle or doesn't quite get there, the next few guys have it. That's how we practice, and that's how we play. We always want to bring it from the practice to the field."

The Ravens did several interesting things over the years that helped the defense stay so tough to beat. They drafted or brought in a number of very good players who'd stay with the team for longer stretches. Or they would develop people who'd been role players at other places—or would have been—into strong, top-notch performers. Much of the defense was built around Ray Lewis, of course, but they could offer lots of talent and they've done a good job of keeping things the same.

"I think a lot of it has to do with the system," said former linebacker Brad Jackson, a member of the 2000 Super Bowl team. "Whenever they change coordinators [on defense], the replacement has pretty much always been there. It's just the continuity of the system and them actually finding players who work well in the system."

Aside from Lewis, here's a list of other members of the Baltimore defense who have earned trips to the Super Bowl in the team's first 21 years of existence: McCrary, Adams, Boulware, McAlister, Thomas, Ed Reed, Terrell Suggs, Bart Scott, Brendan Ayanbadejo, Haloti Ngata, Elvis Dumervil, C.J. Mosley, and Eric Weddle.

That's a long list. But the Ravens kept bringing in people like Reed—a certain Hall of Famer who might be the best safety ever to play the game—so the defense, if it didn't get stronger each year, at least stayed near a certain level. And the players who were part of that unit expected that.

"We just had that tradition feel here like [you have] at certain colleges," Reed said at his retirement press conference. "You just have that feel that you just don't get other places. Like I said, I went to other places. I know how it is out there to some degree. You can tell when guys come here and play here. They leave here knowing that they were part of something. It's not like you were here and it was a job."

What was interesting is several players who found success on the Ravens defense went to other places thanks to free agency and never came close to that kind of success again. A lot of what the Ravens do well on defense stems from the strong play of the line-backers. They roam the field making plays. When the Ravens have been great on defense, they've really had some shutdown corners. Now in recent years, they've struggled a bit in that area, and with pass-rushing—something they're trying to improve for the 2017 season.

In the end, though, everything on the defense, including its reputation, began with Ray Lewis. The Ravens were fortunate that other teams considered him too small coming out of college, and he remained available when they picked him late in the first round of the 1996 draft. But even Lewis, the day he announced that the 2012 season would be his last—he said this just before the playoffs began—talked about how many good defensive players were around him. That's why the Ravens have been so good for so long on defense. It wasn't just about Ray Lewis. It was about all the great players on that side of the ball and what the team did with them.

"I was blessed to have Rod Woodson...to have Tony Siragusa," Lewis said that day. "I was blessed to have Rob Burnett, Michael McCrary. I was blessed to have some great guys who took me up under their wing and said, 'This is the way you should pray about life. This is the way you should live life.'"